GUIDE ON THE SIDE

Sequencing Instruction for Self-Regulated Learners

JULIA A. SIMMS

MARZANO
Resources

555 North Morton Street
Bloomington, IN 47404
888.849.0851
FAX: 866.801.1447

email: info@MarzanoResources.com
MarzanoResources.com

Visit **MarzanoResources.com/reproducibles** to download the free reproducibles in this book.

Printed in the United States of America

FSC
www.fsc.org
MIX
Paper | Supporting responsible forestry
FSC® C008955

Library of Congress Cataloging-in-Publication Data

Names: Simms, Julia A. author
Title: Guide on the side : sequencing instruction for self-regulated learners / by Julia A. Simms.
Description: Bloomington, IN : Marzano Resources, [2026] | Includes bibliographical references and index.
Identifiers: LCCN 2025000853 (print) | LCCN 2025000854 (ebook) | ISBN 9781943360987 paperback | ISBN 9781943360994 ebook
Subjects: LCSH: Self-managed learning
Classification: LCC LB1066 .S56 2026 (print) | LCC LB1066 (ebook) | DDC 371.39/4--dc23/eng/20250526
LC record available at https://lccn.loc.gov/2025000853
LC ebook record available at https://lccn.loc.gov/2025000854

Production Team
Publisher: Kendra Slayton
Associate Publisher: Todd Brakke
Acquisitions Director: Hilary Goff
Editorial Director: Laurel Hecker
Art Director: Rian Anderson
Managing Editor: Sarah Ludwig
Copy Chief: Jessi Finn
Production Editor: Paige Duke
Copy Editor: Anne Marie Watkins
Proofreader: Mark Hain
Text and Cover Designer: Abigail Bowen
Content Development Specialist: Amy Rubenstein
Associate Editor: Elijah Oates
Editorial Assistant: Madison Chartier

To Mom and Dad—you taught me how to learn.

ACKNOWLEDGMENTS

Marzano Resources would like to thank the following reviewers:

Doug Crowley
Assistant Principal
DeForest Area High School
DeForest, Wisconsin

John D. Ewald
Educational Consultant
Frederick, Maryland

Kelly Hilliard
GATE Mathematics Instructor (NBCT)
Darrell C. Swope Middle School
Reno, Nevada

Janet Nuzzie
District Intervention Specialist,
K–12 Mathematics
Pasadena ISD
Pasadena, Texas

TABLE OF CONTENTS

ABOUT THE AUTHOR

JULIA A. SIMMS is vice president of Marzano Resources. A former classroom teacher, she now serves on a team that develops research-based books and resources. Her expertise includes effective instruction, learning progressions and proficiency scales, assessment and grading, argumentation and reasoning skills, and literacy development. She has authored or coauthored fifteen books, including *The Marzano Synthesis*, *A Handbook for High Reliability Schools*, *The New Art and Science of Teaching Reading*, *Where Learning Happens*, and *Marzano Mastery Approaches*.

Julia received a bachelor's degree from Wheaton College and master's degrees in educational leadership from Colorado State University and in K–12 literacy from the University of Northern Colorado.

INTRODUCTION

I wanted to write about metacognition. I've always been fascinated with how people think, particularly how they think about their own thoughts, feelings, and actions. Having worked with Robert J. Marzano since 2010, I've had many opportunities to learn about various metacognitive skills and strategies, and I've seen them in action in classrooms, with powerful results. But, as it turns out, metacognition is just one piece (albeit a very important one) in the complex system of self-regulated learning. As researchers Florian Krieger, Roger Azevedo, Arthur C. Graesser, and Samuel Greiff (2022) explained, "Examining the role of metacognition . . . without considering self-regulated learning would be like fishing without a fishing pole" (p. 684).

Self-regulated learning is an overarching label that encompasses four distinct learning systems: (1) the knowledge system, (2) the cognitive system, (3) the metacognitive system, and (4) the motivational system (Donker, de Boer, Kostons, Dignath van Ewijk, & van der Werf, 2014). Self-regulated learning requires the ability to think metacognitively, and during self-regulated learning, metacognition operates on knowledge and cognition within the context of motivation (Hoyle & Dent, 2018). Try as I might, I couldn't find a compelling way to disentangle metacognition and treat it in isolation. So, I decided to embrace all of self-regulated learning.

Self-regulated learning has the potential to transform education for at least four reasons.

1. **Self-regulated learning enables human agency:** Students have more options than ever before; the amount of information available and the pace of communication are potentially overwhelming. Regardless of their career path, students need to be able to consider their goals, select a course of action, pay attention to whether they achieved their goals,

and adjust if needed. The exercise of these self-regulatory processes is the foundation of what Albert Bandura (2016) called *agency*.

2. **Self-regulated learning amplifies the impact of school:** Time—particularly instructional time—is a precious resource in schools (Organisation for Economic Co-operation and Development, 2023). In many cases, one teacher supports the learning of twenty or more students. When students self-regulate their learning by, for example, persisting when difficulties arise or identifying gaps in their understanding and making plans to close those gaps, they can more effectively utilize the limited time available.
3. **Self-regulated learning facilitates learning from hypermedia:** Computer-based learning environments—featuring hyperlinks, video, audio, and multiple representations of information—are nonlinear and often self-paced (Baars, Wijnia, & Paas, 2017). Students must sequence their examination of informational sources, decide how much time to spend with a particular representation of information, and notice and address comprehension breakdowns. Educational scholar Daniel C. Moos (2018) called self-regulated learning a "critical variable" for learning in technology-based environments (p. 244).
4. **Self-regulated learning redefines educational roles and responsibilities:** Self-regulated learning puts the learner in charge of their learning, including the goal-setting process. Learners' goals "are not necessarily transparent or aligned with task goals or objectives set by others. . . . Poor alignment between learner and instructor goals should not be equated with poor self-regulation" (Hadwin, Järvelä, & Miller, 2018, p. 84). Thus, self-regulated learning requires conversation and negotiation between teachers and students to achieve alignment in the aims of formal education and the goals of individual students (Hulbig, 2023).

Despite these compelling reasons to explore self-regulated learning, writing about it was intimidating at first. You see, self-regulated learning is a big, multifaceted thing. It involves complex relationships between multiple aspects of the self (including motivation, emotions, and beliefs), metacognitive and cognitive processes, and the nature of knowledge. It addresses core elements of human functioning, such as self-efficacy, and involves a complex interplay of personal, behavioral, and environmental factors (Usher & Schunk, 2018). Are you overwhelmed yet?

Don't be. We're going to explore self-regulated learning one element at a time over the next five chapters. In chapter 1, I break down the concept of self-regulation into its component parts and review the research on the relationship between self-regulated learning and academic achievement. Additionally, I present an instructional sequence that you can use to teach students strategies for each element of self-regulated learning. Chapters 2 through 5 will each focus on one of the important elements of self-regulated learning: knowledge (chapter 2), cognition (chapter 3), metacognition (chapter 4), and motivation (chapter 5). For each element, I highlight relevant research and element-specific strategies that you can teach students using the instructional sequence I describe in chapter 1.

Throughout the book, I offer examples of strategies that you can use to promote self-regulated learning relative to knowledge, cognition, metacognition, and motivation. Please accept these strategies as suggestions that have a high probability of leading to the desired outcomes because of the research supporting them. Please do not interpret them as rules or requirements. As educational psychologist Philip H. Winne (2018) explained, research-based strategies represent "heuristics for practices rather than unbending, must-do rules" (p. 45). The online *Cambridge Dictionary* defines *heuristic* as "arriving at a solution by trying different actions to see if they produce the result that is wanted, rather than using strict rules" (Heuristic, n.d.). I will describe the specific self-regulated learning results that are wanted (based on the research) and suggest strategies (actions) that are likely to produce those results. It is your responsibility—and, because this is self-regulated learning, it is also your students' responsibility—to see whether these strategies produce the desired result in your classroom. One of the best ways to do that is through action research.

You and your students can use an *action-research process*, such as the following, to ensure that the strategies you select result in the responses you desire.

1. **Clearly articulate your desired outcome:** For example, research by Heidi L. Andrade and Margaret Heritage (2018) indicated that students need to engage with their goals and be acquainted with the criteria they need to meet to achieve those goals.
2. **Select a strategy that has a high probability of leading to that desired outcome:** For example, in chapter 2 (page 25), I suggest the strategy of articulating learning progressions for knowledge items. Research on rubrics supports the use of this strategy to achieve the desired outcome of engagement with goals and achievement criteria.

3. **Determine how you can collect data on your desired outcome:** For example, you could collect data on students' level of engagement with their goals using a questionnaire or interviews with students. Students could collect data on their level of engagement with their goals using journal entries.
4. **Collect preassessment data on your desired outcome:** For example, if you are doing action research, you would ask students to fill out your questionnaire or you would interview students before teaching them the strategy of articulating learning progressions for knowledge items. If students are doing action research, they could complete several journal entries before learning the strategy of articulating learning progressions for knowledge items.
5. **Learn and use the strategy:** For example, using the guidance in chapter 2 (page 25), you and your students learn to articulate learning progressions for knowledge items.
6. **Collect postassessment data on your desired outcome:** For example, students fill out the questionnaire again or complete a second round of interviews or several more journal entries.
7. **Analyze the data:** Did your selected strategy lead to increases in your desired outcome?
    - If yes, congratulations! The strategy you selected works in your context with your students. Continue to use it.
    - If no, ask why it didn't work.
        - Was your implementation flawed? If so, adjust your implementation and try the strategy again (that is, go back to step 4 of the process with your revised implementation of the strategy).
        - Is the strategy a bad match for your desired outcome? If so, select a different strategy (that is, go back to step 2 of the process).

This approach is similar to a *correlational study*. That is, it measures the correlation (the association) between your use of a specific strategy and your desired outcome.

If you would like to use a more sophisticated approach to action research, you could consider identifying two pre-existing groups of students, learning and using the strategy with one group but not the other, and then comparing preassessment and postassessment data to see if the strategy produced greater gains in the group using the strategy compared to the group not using the strategy. As educational researcher Keith J. Topping (2024) explained, the advantage of this type of *quasi-experimental* approach is that it allows you to isolate the effects of your strategy use from other variables; for example, "you can see whether any improvement could be explained just by students becoming older and more mature" (p. 209).

The two groups should be as alike as possible: the same grade level learning the same content of a similar size with a similar range of ability levels and somewhat similar gender balance. Use the action-research process I articulated previously with both groups, but skip step 5 with the group not using the strategy. The group using the strategy is called the *experimental group*. The group not using the strategy is called the *control group*. During step 7, determine whether the control group or experimental group grew more between pre- and postassessment. If the experimental group grew more, your strategy is working! If the control group grew more, refer to the bullets under step 7 to plan your next steps.

As we explore self-regulated learning together, you will notice that the processes that students use during self-regulated learning mirror this type of action-research process in many ways, albeit much more informally. This is not a coincidence. Self-regulated learning and action research go hand in hand, and your engagement in action research is an effective way to model your own self-regulated learning as you seek to improve your professional learning and practice.

Self-regulated learning is a lifelong endeavor. Thank you for getting your students started with it as soon as possible!

CHAPTER 1

SELF-REGULATED LEARNING

The goal is everything when it comes to self-regulation. As researchers Michael Inzlicht, Kaitlyn M. Werner, Julia L. Briskin, and Brent W. Roberts (2021) wrote:

> Self-regulation can be thought of as an umbrella term that includes a wide array of goal-relevant activities, such as deciding which goal to pursue, planning how to pursue it, implementing these plans, shielding goals from competing concerns, and sometimes even abandoning goals. (p. 321)

There are all kinds of different goals. For example, people aim to achieve "specific desired behaviors (e.g., physical exercise), thoughts or attitudes (e.g., being compassionate), or emotional states (e.g., being content)" (Inzlicht et al., 2021, p. 321). This book is focused on self-regulation toward educational goals—hence the term self-regulated *learning*.

Self-regulated learning is a process. In its simplest form, it has five steps.

1. Set goals.
2. Make plans.
3. Execute plans.
4. Monitor results.
5. Make adjustments.

But that list is deceptively linear, and there's a lot involved in each of those steps. Moving through the process is more like dancing than walking. Researchers Tingting Wang and Susanne P. Lajoie (2023) explained that self-regulated learning "is a dynamic process characterized by phases or subprocesses that evolve over time in a non-linear and recursive manner" (p. 6). Self-regulated learners apply the steps of the process in the general order shown, but they also sometimes skip steps, go backward and revisit previous steps, redo a step after receiving feedback during later steps, tinker with the details of a step, and so on.

In this chapter, I outline the basic research and theories that define and support self-regulation. The theories—the models that various researchers have articulated to describe what goes on during self-regulated learning—help us understand the elements of self-regulated learning and how to help students use them productively. The research—evidence that self-regulated learning promotes students' achievement and well-being in school—speaks to why self-regulated learning is worth teaching and which interventions have the greatest probability of encouraging its growth and development in students. Finally, I explore aspects of instruction for self-regulated learning, including explicit instruction, modeling, practice, and guidance.

Models of Self-Regulated Learning

In the 1950s and 1960s, memory researchers noticed something interesting. Despite being unable to recall previously studied information, people confidently asserted that the information existed in their memory—they just couldn't access it at the moment. Dubbed the *tip-of-the-tongue phenomenon* by Joseph Truman Hart (1965, 1967) and others, these observations led Thomas O. Nelson and Louis Narens (1990) to suggest that humans process information on at least two different levels: (1) the object level and (2) the meta level. At the *object level,* we think directly about information that we're learning, but at the *meta level,* we think about our thinking, including the contents of our memory. In the tip-of-the-tongue phenomenon, the meta level is functioning perfectly: We are aware that certain information is in our memory. There's just a glitch at the object level: We can't produce the desired information right at that moment. This idea—that we think on two levels—laid the foundation for self-regulated learning theory.

Building on earlier work, Bandura (1986) pointed out that when we think on the meta level, we're actually engaging in three things.

1. **Self-observation:** Self-observation involves noticing what we're doing relative to a specific goal. For example, if my goal is to be able to accurately solve a specific type of mathematics problem 90 percent of

the time, self-observation might involve counting how many practice problems I've solved so far and how many are correct.

2. **Self-judgment:** Self-judgment involves comparing our performance against a standard. For example, self-judgment involves recognizing that I have only solved 50 percent of the practice problems correctly so far.
3. **Self-reactions:** Self-reactions involve what we think and how we feel as a result of our self-judgments. For example, if I recognize that I've only solved 50 percent of the practice problems correctly, I might consequently feel discouraged but decide to continue practicing.

Bandura (1997) was particularly interested in how meta-level thinking impacts our beliefs about whether we are good at something—a concept called *self-efficacy*, which I discuss further in chapter 5 (page 111).

These two foundational pieces—Nelson and Narens's (1990) observation that we think at the object and meta levels and Bandura's (1986) description of how we think at the meta level—led to the articulation of five prominent models of self-regulated learning over the next few decades. Table 1.1 summarizes the phases and systems involved in the most recent version of each model.

As table 1.1 illustrates, these models have differences. For example, researcher Monique Boekaerts's (2017) model used a general description of phases compared to the more specific descriptions in Paul R. Pintrich's (2000) and Barry J. Zimmerman's (2013) models. The systems in Winne's (2018) model were significantly different

TABLE 1.1: Prominent Models of Self-Regulated Learning

Model	Phases	Systems Involved
Pintrich, 2000	1. Forethought, planning, and activation 2. Monitoring 3. Control 4. Reaction and reflection	• Cognitive • Motivation or affect • Behavior • Context
Zimmerman, 2013	1. Forethought 2. Performance 3. Self-reflection	• Self • Behavior • Environment
Boekaerts, 2017	1. Protecting learning goals from other goals 2. Steering and directing the learning process 3. Processing information	• Knowledge • Cognition • Metacognition • Motivation

continued →

Model	Phases	Systems Involved
Efklides et al., 2018	1. Goal setting 2. Monitoring 3. Performance 4. Reflection	Person: • Self-concept • Affect • Motivation • Ability • Beliefs Task: • Cognition • Metacognition • Regulation
Winne, 2018	1. Surveying task conditions and context 2. Setting goals and drafting plans 3. Enacting plans and making minor adjustments 4. Reviewing and revamping overall approach	• Conditions • Operations • Products • Evaluations • Standards

from those articulated in the other models. Nevertheless, there are important similarities among the models. Minna Puustinen and Lea Pulkkinen (2001) and Ernesto Panadero (2017) identified the same three overarching phases in all self-regulated learning models: (1) preparatory, (2) performance, and (3) appraisal. Additionally, in all models, self-regulated learning has the characteristics listed in table 1.2.

We will use the four elements in the last row of table 1.2—knowledge, cognition, metacognition, and motivation—to structure our exploration of self-regulated learning in subsequent chapters. Before we begin this exploration, let's review why self-regulated learning deserves your attention.

Research on Self-Regulated Learning

There is plenty of research demonstrating the positive effects of self-regulated learning interventions on motivation, cognition, metacognition, and academic achievement. Table 1.3 (page 12) lists five meta-analyses involving K–12 students that support this assertion.

Beyond the meta-analyses in table 1.3, it is noteworthy that several meta-analyses have also demonstrated the positive effects of self-regulated learning in higher education (Broadbent & Poon, 2015; Jansen, van Leeuwen, Janssen, Jak, & Kester, 2019;

TABLE 1.2: Characteristics of Self-Regulated Learning

Characteristic	Supporting Research
Is goal driven	de Ruig et al., 2023; Elhusseini et al., 2022; Kim et al., 2023; Omarchevska et al., 2022a, 2022b; Wang & Lajoie, 2023
Progresses through phases	de Ruig et al., 2023; Dignath et al., 2023; Hadwin, 2021; Kim et al., 2023; Moos, 2018; Omarchevska et al., 2022b; Oudman et al., 2022; Panadero, 2017; Schuster et al., 2023; Stebner et al., 2022; Zheng et al., 2023
Is cyclical	Dignath et al., 2023; Kim et al., 2023; Omarchevska et al., 2022a, 2022b; Panadero, 2017; Stebner et al., 2022; Wang & Lajoie, 2023; Zheng et al., 2023
Is influenced by context	Moos, 2018; Zheng et al., 2023
Involves monitoring and directing thoughts, feelings, and actions	Azevedo et al., 2018; de Ruig et al., 2023; Dignath et al., 2023; Elhusseini et al., 2022; Kim et al., 2023; McClelland et al., 2023; Moos, 2018; Omarchevska et al., 2022a, 2022b; Oudman et al., 2022; Stebner et al., 2022; Syal & Nietfeld, 2022; van der Graaf et al., 2022; Wang & Lajoie, 2023; Xu et al., 2023; Zhang et al., 2022
Involves knowledge, cognition, metacognition, and motivation	Azevedo et al., 2018; de Ruig et al., 2023; Dignath et al., 2023; Donker et al., 2014; Gutierrez de Blume, 2022; McClelland et al., 2023; Moos, 2018; Omarchevska et al., 2022a, 2022b; Schuster et al., 2023; Stebner et al., 2022; Syal & Nietfeld, 2022; van der Graaf et al., 2022; Wang & Lajoie, 2023; Xu et al., 2023; Zheng et al., 2023

Schneider & Preckel, 2017; Theobald, 2021). There are three interesting nuances in the self-regulated learning research to be aware of.

1. **Time:** Researchers Charlotte Dignath, Reyn van Ewijk, Franziska Perels, and Sabine Fabriz (2023) found that "the effectiveness of [self-regulated learning] training did not increase with the length of the intervention" (p. 36). In fact, they found the opposite to be true: "Shorter intervention led to larger effects" (p. 36). This means that if you don't have a lot of time to dedicate to self-regulated learning, that's OK. Go ahead and give it a little bit of time; it's still worth doing.
2. **Training:** Researchers Sohayla A. Elhusseini, Clair M. Tischner, Kathleen B. Aspiranti, and Alicia L. Fedewa (2022) found that, when given simple instructions on how to implement a self-regulated learning intervention, untrained teachers produced better effects than trained interventionists.

TABLE 1.3: Meta-Analytic Results for Self-Regulated Learning Interventions

Meta-Analysis	Number of Studies	Number of Effect Sizes	Number of Students	Average Effect Size Across All Variables	Effect Sizes for Specific Variables
Dignath et al., 2008	48	263	Not reported	0.69	0.76 for motivation 0.73 for cognitive and metacognitive strategy use 0.62 for academic performance
Dignath & Büttner, 2008	74	357	8,619	0.69	0.71 for grades 7–10 0.68 for grades 1–6
Donker et al., 2014	58	180	Not reported	0.66	1.25 in writing 0.73 in science 0.66 in mathematics 0.36 in reading
Li et al., 2018	59 (all studies conducted in China with Chinese students)	264	23,497	0.44	0.44 in science 0.29 in language 0.59 in others
Elhusseini et al., 2022	46	150	5,255	0.83	1.01 in reading^{ns} 0.82 in writing^{ns} 0.38 in mathematics

^{ns} = not significant at the 0.05 level

They hypothesized, "It could be that untrained individuals had more flexibility in how they adapted the intervention in order to individualize to children's needs" (p. 1132). This means that you—rather than a university researcher or expert—are the very best person to teach your students about self-regulated learning. Sometimes less is more when you're trying to explain a complex concept to a novice learner.

3. **Age:** As researchers Niels J. de Ruig, Peter F. de Jong, and Marjolein Zee (2023) stated, "Elementary school students are able to regulate their learning effectively on a basic level" (p. 71). Megan M. McClelland, Ahmad Ahmadi, and Shannon B. Wanless (2023) highlighted interventions that have "significantly improved behavioral self-regulation and academic achievement in preschool children, with effects especially strong for low-income children" (p. 180). It is never too early to start using self-regulated learning interventions. Whether you teach kindergarten or twelfth grade, self-regulated learning will benefit your students.

It is also important to understand the nature of highly effective self-regulated learning. Specifically, when students have highly developed self-regulated learning skills, those skills are often executed automatically, and they are transferable to a wide variety of learning situations. These two concepts—automaticity and transfer—are critical to a basic understanding of self-regulated learning, so we'll take a closer look at each.

Automaticity

Highly self-regulated learners enact self-regulated learning skills unconsciously; they only give conscious attention to regulating their learning when something surprising or unexpected occurs, such as a breakdown in comprehension or an error. This means that the very best self-regulated learning requires no conscious regulation at all—it runs on autopilot unless something goes wrong. Expert self-regulated learners have honed their skills in knowledge, cognition, metacognition, and motivation so extensively that those skills have become habits. When they're learning, they're simply allowing their automatic responses to invisibly guide their actions. Here's how Winne (2018) explained it:

> After extensive practice, learned processes become automated. Automated processes are carried out rapidly, they reliably produce intended results and typically "run off" without one's noticing. If one tries to disassemble an automated process, the process often shows a dramatic reduction in pace and may even spawn errors. (p. 37)

The goal of self-regulated learning interventions is for students to practice self-regulated learning processes so extensively that they become habits and function in the background during learning, only entering consciousness when students need to use them to fix a problem or correct an error.

To understand how automaticity develops and functions, it is helpful to understand the interactions among working memory, long-term memory, and perception during learning. Figure 1.1 illustrates these relationships.

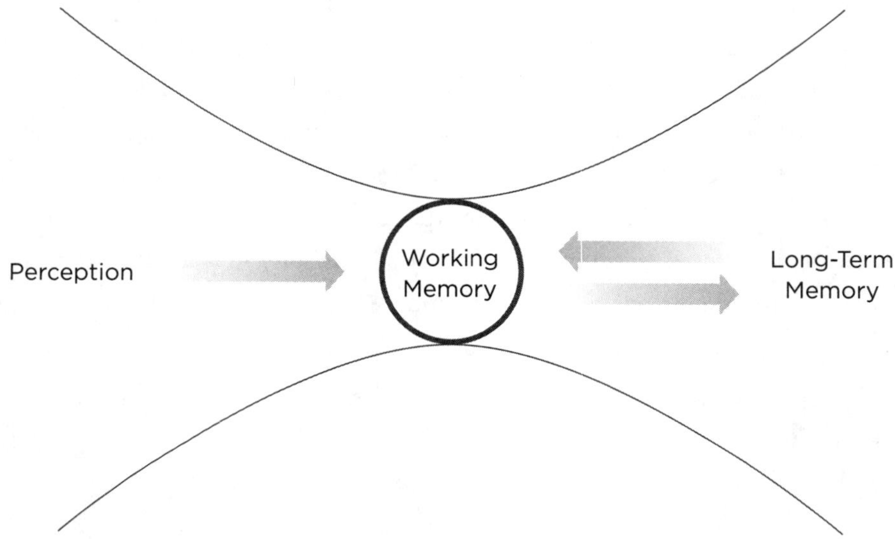

Source: Simms, 2025, p. 71.

FIGURE 1.1: Relationships among working memory, long-term memory, and perception.

Working memory, as shown in the middle of figure 1.1, is the center of consciousness where most learning happens. As John Sweller (2022) explained, whatever is in working memory is what you are thinking about at the moment. Critically, working memory is limited in capacity. It can only hold and productively work with a modicum of information; too much information overwhelms its capacity and inhibits learning. Working memory draws information from both perception (inputs from the world around us) and long-term memory. Long-term memory is where we store information we have already learned. Once information is in working memory, it is ideally organized, connected to related information in long-term memory, and moved to long-term memory for storage until it is retrieved back into working memory for further use or refinement.

When students consciously enact self-regulated learning skills, they are using working memory; they combine their perceptions of a learning task with the skills they have previously learned and stored in long-term memory. This is an effective way to regulate one's learning, but it is not the most efficient way.

When students have practiced self-regulated learning skills to the point of automaticity, they are able to activate and use those skills *without consuming working memory*. This bypass is made possible by the cognitive process of *resonance*. As researchers Joachim Wirth, Ferdinand Stebner, Melanie Trypke, Corinna Schuster, and Detlev Leutner (2020) explained, resonance "is likely to happen if sensory information matches long-term memory information" (p. 1130). For example, if a student has learned the cognitive skill of examining relationships to automaticity, resonance will activate that skill automatically in situations where it is appropriate. A kindergartner might automatically identify similarities and differences when presented with two versions of the same story. A middle schooler might automatically see similarities and differences between linear equations and quadratic functions. A high schooler might automatically identify similarities and differences between DNA and RNA.

Metacognitive skills can also be activated through resonance. For example, a student who has learned the metacognitive skills of goal setting, planning, and reflection may automatically activate them when confronted with a familiar type of text. Speaking from the student's perspective, Wirth and colleagues (2020) explained, "If you expect yourself to [be] able to easily understand the text . . . you will probably start reading the text in the way you usually read this kind of text without engaging in careful and conscious planning" (p. 1136). If the student's experience reading the new text matches the expectations they formed from previous experiences, they don't need to engage conscious monitoring and control processes. However, if the student encounters textual elements, vocabulary, sentence constructions, or other features that do not match their expectations—that do not resonate with long-term memory—they will ideally activate working memory (which will slow down their reading speed) and consciously use self-regulated learning skills (such as rereading, diagramming, or paraphrasing) to preserve their comprehension.

Essentially, a student who has learned self-regulation skills—and practiced them until they can be performed automatically—has enabled their long-term memory to scan perception for situations that match their automatic skills. When long-term memory senses a match, it simply activates the appropriate skills, without recourse to working memory. This is an extraordinarily efficient way to learn and helps explain the powerful effects of self-regulated learning on motivation, cognition, metacognition, and academic achievement.

Transfer

In addition to automaticity, highly effective self-regulated learning skills are transferable. *Transferable* means that "learning in one context enhances performance in a different context" (Schuster et al., 2023, p. 2). As psychologist Sarah Shi Hui Wong (2023) explained, transferable skills have been a "holy grail" sought after for over a century (p. 16). In the early 1900s, many people believed that learning subjects such as Latin and Greek would generally improve students' minds and make them better at other, unrelated subjects (Mayer, 2023). This belief was one of the justifications for including Latin and Greek in the curriculum at that time. The idea that knowledge about one subject can make you better at another, unrelated subject is called *general transfer*, and evidence has shown that it doesn't happen. In fact, research by psychologists Edward L. Thorndike and Robert S. Woodworth (Thorndike, 1931; Thorndike & Woodworth, 1901) showed that students who learned Latin and students who did not learn Latin performed equally well on mathematics tasks, and subsequent research produced similar results (for example, Singley & Anderson, 1989).

Despite the ineffectiveness of general transfer, skills exist that do transfer between different tasks, and even between different subject areas. (We will discuss many of these transferable skills in our discussion of self-regulated learning.) For example, a student who has learned to use the cognitive strategy of concept mapping to organize information from text passages in English language arts can use the same concept-mapping strategy to organize information from text passages in social studies. Or, a student who has learned to use metacognitive skills to plan, monitor, and adjust their performance on an experimentation task in science can use the same metacognitive skills to plan, monitor, and adjust their performance on a historical investigation task in social studies. These are examples of a successful transfer of self-regulated learning skills.

For transfer to occur, there are three preconditions, according to Wong (2023).

1. Students must recognize that previously learned knowledge is relevant to a new task.
2. Students must correctly recall the previously learned knowledge.
3. Students must effectively apply the previously learned knowledge in the new context.

Step 1 is easier when the new task is structurally similar to the task in which the student learned the transferable skill (as in the concept-mapping example; both tasks involved reading a text). This is called *near transfer*. Step 1 is more difficult when the new task is structurally different from the task in which the student learned the transferable skill (as in the metacognitive example; experimentation tasks are structurally different from investigation tasks). This is called *far transfer* (Stebner et al., 2022). Therefore, you can help students during step 1 (especially when the new task involves far transfer) by prompting them to think about how previously learned skills might apply to a new task. Such prompts are classified as guidance and, ideally, occur within a holistic system of self-regulated learning skills instruction. I will close this chapter by describing such a system.

Instruction for Self-Regulated Learning

Self-regulated learning skills must be explicitly taught and explicitly learned. According to educational scholar Jeffrey A. Greene (2021), "The various processes of self-regulated learning are not intuitive or innate" (p. 652). Researchers Ellen L. Usher and Dale H. Schunk (2018) clearly stated that "most self-regulation skills do not arise on their own" (p. 25). Given that self-regulated learning skills do not develop spontaneously, you will need to provide explicit instruction and opportunities for guided practice and feedback if you want students to acquire and use self-regulated learning skills.

Research supports the need for explicit instruction of self-regulated learning skills. In 2021, Charlotte Dignath and Marcel V. J. Veenman reviewed seventeen studies of self-regulated learning instruction involving 541 teachers and 2,318 students that were published between 1992 and 2019. They found that, in many classrooms, self-regulated learning instruction unfortunately happens only implicitly, meaning that "teachers prompted [self-regulated learning] rather indirectly by creating learning environments that required students to regulate their learning" (p. 521). This type of implicit instruction is ineffective. Dignath and Veenman (2021) reported that "no, or even negative, associations were found between learning environments that were supposed to activate [self-regulated learning] and students' learning outcomes, if no strategy instruction took place" (p. 521). In contrast, students whose teachers provided explicit instruction on self-regulated learning strategies were more likely to actually use the skills they had learned: "All studies found a positive association between the amount of teachers' instruction of self-regulation strategies and students' use of self-regulation strategies" (Dignath & Veenman, 2021, p. 521). Based on their review, Dignath and Veenman (2021) described what explicit instruction involves: "Explicit instruction means that the teacher *clearly instructs the students about a strategy* by explaining and *demonstrating how to execute a particular strategy*, clarifying benefits of strategy use, *and supporting students in strategy application*" (p. 494; emphasis added).

As seen here, providing opportunities for students to practice and refine self-regulated learning strategies is necessary. When preceded by explicit explanations from the teacher about specific strategies—including how to execute them, when to use them, and why they are helpful—opportunities for guided practice are essential for effective self-regulated learning instruction. Therefore, teach self-regulated learning strategies using the following instructional sequence.

1. Explicit instruction
2. Modeling
3. Practice
4. Guidance

This sequence incorporates the characteristics of effective self-regulated learning instruction Dignath and Veenman (2021) identified and mirrors the flow of effective self-regulated learning instruction Greene and colleagues (2015) identified in their literature review. Greene and colleagues (2015) found that among effective teachers of self-regulated learning skills, "direct or explicit instruction was often used to teach new [self-regulated learning] concepts, knowledge, and skills to students. Then, instructors often modeled these strategies for the students. After that, guided practice was employed" (p. 97). In the following section, I review each step of the instructional sequence in a general way. Then, in chapters 2 through 5, I explain how to use the sequence to teach specific strategies associated with knowledge, cognition, metacognition, and motivation.

Explicit Instruction

Students need explicit instruction about self-regulated learning strategies for several reasons. As I articulated, the main reason is that research has unequivocally shown that explicit instruction results in greater and more effective strategy use than more implicit instructional approaches. But students also need explicit instruction so they understand when to use the strategies and how they benefit from using them, which, in turn, contributes to their motivation for using them, as I discuss in chapter 5 (page 111). Explicit instruction of self-regulated learning strategies should involve the following.

- **What:** Name of the strategy being taught
- **When:** Description and examples of when to use the strategy
- **Why:** Description and examples of why the strategy is helpful
- **How:** Steps of the strategy being taught

Dignath and Veenman (2021) referred to this as the *WWW&H rule*. For example, one of the strategies that I present in chapter 3 (page 47) is retrieval practice. As a preview, that strategy's WWW&H is as follows.

- **What:** Retrieval practice
- **When:** Acquiring new knowledge
- **Why:** Retrieving knowledge from your memory results in better learning than simply restudying that knowledge.
- **How:** Use the following process.
    a. Identify the new knowledge that you need to acquire.
    b. Expose yourself to the new knowledge (for example, by reading a text, watching a video, or observing a demonstration).
    c. Attempt to reproduce the knowledge without using any resources.
    d. Use resources to evaluate your reproduction of the knowledge, and identify incorrect or missing elements.
    e. Repeat steps c. and d. until you are able to reproduce the knowledge accurately and reliably (for example, a certain number of times in a row without errors).

The strategy's WWW&H lays the foundation that students need to take full advantage of the next step: modeling.

Modeling

After presenting students with the steps of the strategy being taught, provide opportunities for them to watch someone else perform the strategy. One option is to model the strategy using a think-aloud to make your thoughts apparent to students. For example, when you model retrieval practice, begin by verbally identifying the new knowledge you need to acquire. Think aloud about whether the new knowledge is information (such as a set of facts and vocabulary terms) or a process (such as a set of steps to follow). Then, expose yourself to the new knowledge. If you are reading a text, read the text aloud. If you are watching a video or demonstration, ensure students can see and hear it too. While reading or watching, think aloud about what information or which steps of the process seem most important.

Then, put all resources away and try to reproduce what you saw either by writing or speaking. (If you are speaking, record what you say so you can revisit it during the fourth step.) You could also generate a list of questions about the knowledge and try to answer the questions without resources. Think aloud about what you remember and what you cannot remember. For example, "I remember there was a term used to describe that group of people, but I can't remember the term" or "I remember that the third step is important because if you get it wrong, it ruins the rest of the process."

Finally, use resources to evaluate your reproduction of the knowledge. For each element that you remembered accurately, verbally celebrate your performance. For each element that you forgot or remembered wrong, note the omission or error. Think aloud about how you feel about these errors and omissions so students can see that negative feelings are a normal part of the process. Finally, decide how well you will need to perform before you terminate the practice cycle; for example, "I need to be able to reproduce descriptions of nine vocabulary terms and five facts accurately at least three times in a row" or "I need to be able to write out all six steps of this process, with examples of each step, at least four times in a row" or "I need to answer all of these questions correctly at least twice in a row."

Another option for modeling is to use videos of other adults or (even better) students modeling the strategy. (After you have implemented self-regulated learning for multiple years, you can build your own library of students' videos modeling the strategies.) Researchers found that using video modeling examples improved student outcomes, especially on similar tasks (near transfer; Raaijmakers, Baars, Paas, van Merriënboer, & van Gog, 2018; Raaijmakers, Baars, Schaap, Paas, & van Merriënboer, 2018). A 2022 study found similar results, and added that "the benefits were found despite the rather short instruction time of the video modeling examples (10 min)" (Omarchevska, Lachner, Richter, & Scheiter, 2022a, p. 1054). If you use video modeling examples, pause the video at intervals and ensure that students are aware of what the person in the video is likely thinking, especially if the person in the video is not thinking aloud. (If you make your own video library, specify that students should think aloud when they record their videos.)

Practice

Students need multiple opportunities to practice a strategy once they are familiar with its steps and have observed others performing it. In fact, Winne (2022) argued that self-regulated learning is a form of expertise that requires *deliberate practice*. According to psychology researchers K. Anders Ericsson and Kyle W. Harwell (2019), deliberate practice has five important criteria.

1. Training by a teacher
2. Internal representation of the goal based on teacher demonstrations
3. Practice activities to attain the goal

4. Immediate feedback on attempts
5. Ability to repeatedly revise attempts to gradually approach the desired performance

This kind of deliberate practice "allows students to discover more efficient and refined forms of strategies" (Hoyle & Dent, 2018, p. 51). The first two phases of our instructional sequence, explicit instruction and modeling, address the first two criteria for deliberate practice. This phase, practice, addresses the third and fifth criteria, and the next phase, guidance, provides the feedback students need.

As you've read, self-regulated learning requires both skill and will. Psychologist Deanna Kuhn (2022) explained, competence "is a prerequisite but . . . not a sufficient condition" (p. 79) for self-regulated learning to occur. Students may "have the competence to exercise [self-regulated learning skills] but it will count for little if one lacks the disposition to do so" (Kuhn, 2022, p. 73). Therefore, an important goal of the practice phase of the sequence is for strategies to become automatic. Recall that when students learn a skill to automaticity, they use it without consciously thinking about it. They no longer need to choose it because it is automatically activated and executed straight from long-term memory through resonance; it consumes no working-memory resources. The only way for a skill or strategy to become automatic is through repeated practice. You can encourage this kind of repeated practice by seeking to embed practice of self-regulated learning strategies in every activity of the school day.

For example, identify all situations in which students need to remember information, and prompt them to use retrieval practice. Learning new content knowledge is a clear opportunity, but nonacademic situations offer opportunities as well. Students often need to remember multistep directions for completing assignments or classroom tasks; retrieval practice can help them do that. If you notice that certain classroom routines aren't working because students forget steps or details, you can have them use retrieval practice to solidify the processes in their memory. Students can use retrieval practice to remember what to do during various safety drills (fire, tornado, lockdown). After a school assembly, students can use retrieval practice to remember what happened and any important information that was shared. The more you can prompt students to use a strategy, the more practice they will get with it, and the more likely it is to become automatic.

Guidance

Guidance is the secret ingredient that makes self-regulated learning instruction work. A 2016 study by researchers Ard W. Lazonder and Ruth Harmsen quantitatively synthesized results from seventy-two studies involving the effects of guidance on student learning. Lazonder and Harmsen (2016) found that "guidance has a significant positive effect on . . . learning activities [d = 0.66], performance success [d = 0.71], and learning outcomes [d = 0.50]" (p. 703). Lazonder and Harmsen (2016) identified six specific types of guidance, which fall along a spectrum spanning from specific to general. Novice learners will need more specific guidance, whereas more advanced learners should receive more general guidance. Figure 1.2 shows these types of guidance.

GENERAL

Process Constraint: A resource that reduces the complexity of a learning task; for example, providing a list of options for a student to choose from to make a decision task easier

Status Overview: A road map for a task that denotes where a student currently is; for example, telling a student that they have successfully demonstrated that they can organize content but haven't yet demonstrated their ability to analyze that content

Prompt: A general hint about what a student might do or think about next; for example, asking a student if they have compiled enough information to construct an argument or if they need to gather more

Heuristic: A detailed suggestion about what a student might do or think about next; for example, telling a student that they could consult multiple sources to compare and contrast opposing perspectives on an issue

Scaffold: A tool that structures and supports a specific activity that a student needs to carry out; for example, providing a template for students to fill out as they construct an argument

Explanation: A direct presentation of needed information; for example, if a student lacks necessary prior knowledge or cannot find important information that they need to proceed, directly telling or providing them (such as through video or text) what they need to know to stay on track

SPECIFIC

Source: Adapted from Lazonder & Harmsen, 2016.

FIGURE 1.2: Types of guidance.

Guidance allows students to work on tasks slightly beyond their current level of knowledge or skill; it enables them to focus on the elements of a task they are competent with by assisting with the elements they are not yet able to do. For example, if a student can't use retrieval practice because they can't remember the steps of the process, you might write the steps on a sticky note and put it on their desk. This is an example of a scaffold. However, if a student consistently and correctly uses retrieval practice in a variety of situations but is having trouble with setting a criterion score regarding how many times they need to recall the information accurately to exit the retrieval-practice cycle, you might help them create a simple scale that calibrates the importance of the information with the number of accurate reproductions needed (more important information needs more accurate reproductions and less important information needs fewer accurate reproductions). This is an example of a process constraint.

Summary

I began this chapter by introducing the goal-driven process of self-regulated learning. As I mentioned in the introduction, self-regulated learning may seem like a simple, linear process, but it is actually dynamic, cyclical, recursive, and complex. However, the extant models of self-regulated learning all indicate that it involves four elements: (1) knowledge, (2) cognition, (3) metacognition, and (4) motivation. As students do the self-regulated learning dance, they engage with each of these elements. Ideally, this happens automatically, but this automaticity does not arise innately or intuitively. Instead, you must explicitly teach students strategies for each element, model the strategies, and design environments that provide opportunities for students to practice the strategies with appropriate amounts of guidance. This instructional sequence—explicit instruction, modeling, practice, and guidance—can be applied to the strategies associated with each of the four elements involved in self-regulated learning. In the next chapter, I begin our in-depth exploration of strategies for each element by examining self-regulated learning strategies for knowledge.

CHAPTER 2
KNOWLEDGE

Knowledge is the stuff of education. More technically, your knowledge is all the information and skills stored in your memory (McCarthy & McNamara, 2023), and in terms of education, it is the objective. If students are to engage in self-regulated learning, they first need to understand the nature of knowledge; they need to understand how knowledge works. This can be challenging because, even in educator preparation programs, humans do not often think of knowledge as a system, with categories, processes, and guidelines. But it is (Greene, Sandoval, & Bråten, 2016). Students engaging in self-regulated learning need to understand how to:

1. Identify different kinds of knowledge
2. Learn each kind of knowledge
3. Articulate knowledge items as learning progressions

In this chapter, I begin by exploring the differences between declarative and procedural knowledge, with examples of each. Next, I review how declarative knowledge and procedural knowledge are learned and explain how the learning process between the two types differs. The goal of this first section is to equip you with the knowledge you need to provide explicit instruction to students about how to (1) identify different kinds of knowledge and (2) learn each kind of knowledge. Then, I explore rubrics and suggest a simple way for students to articulate knowledge items (both declarative and procedural) as learning progressions. The goal of this second section is to equip you to model and give students guidance as they (3) articulate knowledge items as learning progressions. Finally, I discuss the assessment and measurement of knowledge. Once students have articulated knowledge items as learning progressions, it is fairly straightforward for you and your students to track their learning and progress.

Declarative and Procedural Knowledge

Knowledge comes in two flavors: declarative and procedural (Mayer, 2023; Winne, 2022). *Declarative knowledge* is things you know, and *procedural knowledge* is things you do.

Declarative knowledge comes in a variety of differently sized chunks. Very small chunks include facts and vocabulary terms, while large, more complex chunks include concepts and generalizations. Here are some examples of the different types of declarative knowledge.

- **Facts:** Simple statements about an idea, such as "The mean of a set of numbers can differ from the median"
- **Vocabulary terms:** Labels for ideas, such as "The *mean* is a measure of central tendency that summarizes a set of numbers"
- **Concepts:** Labels for categories of ideas, such as "*Measures of central tendency* are statistical metrics used to summarize datasets by identifying a single value that represents the center or typical value of the data, such as the mean, median, and mode"
- **Generalizations:** Claims or assertions about an idea or set of ideas, such as "The mean is the best measure of central tendency if the data are symmetrically distributed without outliers"

Notice that all of these examples are things that students know—not things they do. You cannot perform "The mean of a set of numbers can differ from the median"—it is simply something you know. There is a different label for the knowledge of how to do things: procedural knowledge.

Procedural knowledge also comes in differently sized chunks. Strategies and tactics are small chunks, while macroprocesses are large chunks. Here are some examples of procedural knowledge.

- **Strategies:** Sets of actions that are performed in a specific order, such as "how to calculate the mean from a set of values"
- **Tactics:** Sets of actions that are performed in an overall way (rather than in a specific order), such as "how to select the appropriate

measure of central tendency (mean, median, or mode) based on the characteristics of a dataset and the specific context of an analysis"

- **Macroprocesses:** Overarching processes comprised of strategies and tactics, such as "how to collect and analyze a dataset to answer a research question"

As you've read, it is critical for students to understand the differences between declarative and procedural knowledge because they are learned differently. The tasks used to learn declarative knowledge are different from the tasks used to learn procedural knowledge (McCarthy & McNamara, 2023; Wirth et al., 2020). Figure 2.1 shows the progression of learning tasks for declarative and procedural knowledge.

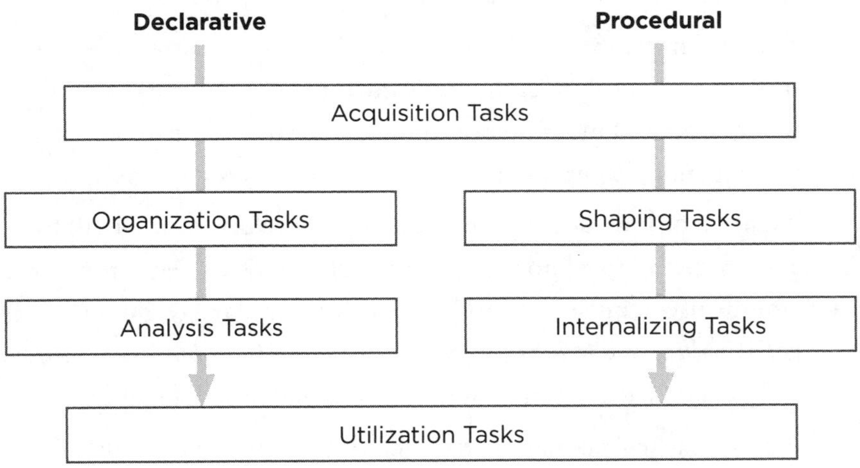

Source: Adapted from Simms, 2025.

FIGURE 2.1: Progression of learning tasks for declarative and procedural knowledge.

First, let's take a closer look at each of the learning tasks for declarative knowledge.

- **Acquisition tasks:** During *acquisition tasks*, students are simply exposed to new knowledge, with the goal of getting new knowledge into their working memory. For declarative knowledge, this might involve reading text, watching a video, or listening to direct instruction.
- **Organization tasks:** After acquisition, declarative knowledge is organized using organization tasks. *Organization tasks* are designed to help students build structures, or *schemas*, that show how various facts, vocabulary terms, and concepts relate to one another. One of the reasons literacy teachers ask students to make connections when reading a text is to promote the organization of declarative knowledge

through schema formation. Recall from the discussion of automaticity in chapter 1 (page 13) that knowledge must be organized to move into long-term memory. The goal of organization tasks is to send organized knowledge into long-term memory.

- **Analysis tasks:** Next, declarative knowledge is analyzed using analysis tasks. *Analysis tasks* bring organized knowledge back into working memory from long-term memory, refine or reorganize it to eliminate misconceptions or errors, and, in many cases, add new knowledge to it. This reorganization usually results in the formation of generalizations. The goal of analysis tasks is to improve the organization and increase the complexity of information in long-term memory.
- **Utilization tasks:** Finally, declarative knowledge can be used in utilization tasks. *Utilization tasks* mirror the complexity of real-world tasks and often involve problem solving, decision making, investigation, experimentation, invention, or systems analysis.

As an example of how declarative knowledge develops through all four types of tasks, consider declarative knowledge for the elementary science topic of plants. A student might use acquisition tasks to learn vocabulary terms such as *plant*, *sunlight*, *water*, *pollinator*, *habitat*, *seed*, *seedling*, *germination*, *photosynthesis*, *soil*, *nutrients*, and *growth*. Facts on this topic might include the following.

- A plant has several main parts, including roots, stems, leaves, flowers, and seeds.
- Plants make their own food using sunlight, water, and carbon dioxide.
- Plants can be found in various habitats, including forests, deserts, grasslands, and wetlands.

Organization tasks for this declarative knowledge would ask the student to show how the vocabulary terms and facts relate to one other. The student could organize the terms and facts into (1) parts of a plant, (2) plant growth, (3) photosynthesis, and (4) habitats of plants. During an analysis task, the student might examine the relationships among the content elements. For example, photosynthesis is a biological process that is facilitated by sunlight and water. The student might also make generalizations about the content, such as that habitats influence which plant parts adapt to survive in those environments. Finally, as a utilization task, the student might plan a garden. They would need to decide where to place the garden, which plants to include, and where to put each type of plant in the garden. They might also decide whether to grow the garden from seeds or seedlings, make plans to protect the garden from animals that might harm it, and figure out how to encourage pollinators and other creatures that could help it flourish. Such a real-world task involves decision making, problem solving, and systems analysis.

Now, let's consider the learning tasks for procedural knowledge.

- **Acquisition tasks:** As I noted, *acquisition tasks* should expose students to new knowledge so it enters their working memory. For procedural knowledge, this often involves watching someone else perform a process or reading or listening to a list of steps associated with a process.
- **Shaping tasks:** Once students have acquired a process, they practice it using shaping tasks. *Shaping tasks* are practice opportunities in which the learner focuses on executing a process with a high level of accuracy. Speed is not the focus of shaping tasks; learners typically execute processes slowly during shaping tasks. During these tasks, it is important to ensure that learners encode the process in long-term memory *without errors*. If students make errors, it is important that they recognize their mistakes and quickly correct them. Because of their focus on accuracy, shaping tasks require a high level of guidance and scaffolding to protect against students' encoding errors while they are learning a process. The goal of shaping tasks is the accurate encoding of a process.
- **Internalizing tasks:** Next, procedural knowledge is the subject of internalizing tasks. *Internalizing tasks* are practice opportunities in which the learner focuses on executing a process accurately while increasing their speed. The goal of internalizing tasks is automaticity (as I described in chapter 1, page 13) or, because many macroprocesses are too complex to be learned to automaticity, *controlled processing*, which means that a learner's execution of a process is easy and smooth despite the need to dedicate some working memory to it.
- **Utilization tasks:** Finally, procedural knowledge, like declarative knowledge, can be used in utilization tasks, which mirror the complexity of real-world tasks and often involve problem solving, decision making, investigation, experimentation, invention, or systems analysis.

As an example of how procedural knowledge develops through all four types of tasks, consider procedural knowledge for the elementary mathematics topic of multiplication. A student might use acquisition tasks to learn the partial products method for multidigit multiplication, as illustrated in the following process.

1. **Understand the problem:** Identify the two multidigit numbers you need to multiply (for example, 23 × 14).
2. **Break down each number:** Break down each number into its place-value components (for example, 23 = 20 + 3 and 14 = 10 + 4).
3. **Multiply each part:** Multiply each part of the first number by each part of the second number (for example, 20 × 10, 20 × 4, 3 × 10, 3 × 4).
4. **Calculate each product:** Perform the multiplication (for example, 20 × 10 = 200, 20 × 4 = 80, 3 × 10 = 30, 3 × 4 = 12).
5. **Add the partial products:** Add all the partial products together (for example, 200 + 80 + 30 + 12 = 322).
6. **Determine the answer:** Write down the sum of the partial products (for example, 23 × 14 = 322).

Shaping tasks for this procedural knowledge would ask the student to repeatedly execute the strategy with a high level of accuracy. For this practice, the student might use a varied set of practice problems that involves, in addition to multidigit multiplication problems, single-digit multiplication problems, place-value and expanded-form problems, addition and subtraction problems, word problems, and basic division problems. Each time the student encounters a multidigit multiplication problem, they practice using the partial products strategy to solve it. As I discuss in chapter 3 (page 47), this type of interleaved practice is very effective for shaping tasks.

As the student gains confidence with the strategy and can perform it without errors, they move on to internalizing tasks. For these tasks, the student solves sets of multidigit multiplication problems as quickly as possible. For example, they might time themself to see how quickly they can solve twenty problems in a row. The next day, they repeat the drill, trying to beat their time from the day before while maintaining high accuracy. As I also discuss in chapter 3 (page 47), this is called *spaced practice*, and it is effective for developing fluency with a process. Finally, as a utilization task, the student plans goody-bag items for a community event for forty-five people. The student uses the partial products multiplication strategy to figure out how many total items are needed if each bag contains thirteen items, what the total cost will be for all the items, and how much space the items will take up if each is packed in a box with a specific volume.

As is hopefully obvious, the order of learning tasks for both kinds of knowledge is important. Students must acquire declarative knowledge before they can organize it, and they must organize it before they can analyze it. Similarly, students must acquire procedural knowledge before they can shape it, and they must shape it before they can internalize it. The terms used in the research literature for knowledge learned during previous learning tasks are *background knowledge* or *prior knowledge*. Prior knowledge is critical for all kinds of learning, especially self-regulated learning. Students who proceed through learning tasks in the appropriate order will have the prior knowledge they need to succeed at each subsequent task. Computer scientist and information engineer Liang-Yi Li (2019) explained:

> Prior knowledge plays a key role in self-regulated learning. High-prior knowledge learners are guided by a more complete conceptual structure and have more cognitive resources to plan and monitor their learning process. Therefore, studies have demonstrated that high-prior knowledge learners exhibit higher levels of cognitive skill in self-regulated processes than low-prior knowledge students do. (p. 417)

One of the major reasons that students need to understand the differences between declarative and procedural knowledge and how they learn each is so they can manage their prior knowledge. They should not do analysis tasks until they have an appropriate amount of declarative knowledge already organized in their long-term memory. Similarly, they should probably not engage in internalizing tasks until they are confident that their execution of a process is accurate (as emphasized during shaping tasks). Attempting utilization tasks without appropriately analyzed and internalized knowledge will likely lead to frustration and, potentially, failure. Students' ability to understand and manage their prior knowledge is foundational to all other self-regulated learning strategies.

I discuss the cognitive strategies associated with each type of learning task—acquisition, organization, analysis, utilization, shaping, and internalizing—in chapter 3 (page 47). For our purposes in this chapter, it is sufficient to know that there are two types of knowledge, declarative and procedural, that are learned using different progressions of learning tasks; the general nature of each type of learning task; and the importance of prior knowledge for the success of subsequent learning tasks. This understanding will help you provide explicit instruction to students regarding how to (1) identify different kinds of knowledge and (2) learn each kind of knowledge.

Those two items themselves constitute declarative knowledge for the knowledge system: They are things students need to know about knowledge. There is also procedural knowledge for the knowledge system, namely how to (3) articulate knowledge items as learning progressions. To understand why this is an important skill, you need to understand the research and theories on rubrics.

Rubrics

An effective rubric articulates two things: (1) criteria and (2) performance levels (Brookhart, 2018). *Criteria* are important aspects of a knowledge item, and *performance levels* describe novice, proficient, and expert manifestations of a knowledge item. A scoring strategy is an additional characteristic of rubrics that was once considered essential (Popham, 1997) but has since been acknowledged to be optional—helpful only in certain situations, and unnecessary or even detrimental in others (Panadero, Jonsson, Pinedo, & Fernández-Castilla, 2023). Rubrics have a substantial research base, which I review briefly in the following section. Then, I explain how students can use the principles of effective rubrics to articulate knowledge items as learning progressions.

Research on Rubrics

Educators have been toying with the idea of rubrics since at least the early 1900s (Hillegas, 1912), but research interest and classroom use increased exponentially after the publication of educator W. James Popham's 1997 article "What's Wrong—and What's Right—With Rubrics" (Dawson, 2017). Table 2.1 lists five major empirical reviews of research on rubrics published since 2000.

As exemplified by the findings in table 2.1, rubrics should be used in a specific way to produce positive outcomes for students. First, rubrics should provide clarity and transparency about what students are expected to learn and how they can demonstrate their learning. Second, rubrics should be designed primarily for (and, ideally, by) students and be used primarily to set goals and provide feedback (and only secondarily for scoring or grading). Third, the way that knowledge is articulated on a rubric (the criteria) should describe, as substantively as possible, the learning that needs to occur and the quality of that learning.

In 2023, researchers Ernesto Panadero, Anders Jonsson, Leire Pinedo, and Belén Fernández-Castilla conducted a meta-analytic review of twenty-three studies to estimate the effects of rubric use on academic performance, self-regulated learning, and self-efficacy. Table 2.2 (page 34) summarizes their findings.

TABLE 2.1: Research Studies on Rubrics

Citation	Number of Studies Reviewed	Findings
Jonsson & Svingby, 2007	75	"Rubrics seem to have the potential of promoting learning and/or improving instruction. The main reason for this potential lies in the fact that rubrics make expectations and criteria explicit, which also facilitates feedback and self-assessment" (p. 130).
Reddy & Andrade, 2010	20	"Simply handing out a rubric cannot be expected to have an impact on student work: students must be taught to actively use a rubric for self- and peer assessments and revision to reap its benefits" (p. 445).
Panadero & Jonsson, 2013	21	"The use of rubrics may mediate improved performance through (a) providing transparency to the assessment, which in turn may (b) reduce student anxiety. The use of rubrics may also (c) aid the feed-back process, (d) improve student self-efficacy, and (e) support student self-regulation; all of which may indirectly facilitate improved student performance" (p. 140).
Brookhart & Chen, 2015	63	"Rubrics that focus on the *requirements for an assignment* and not indications of learning, especially if used in classroom contexts where evaluation is more salient than learning (Stiggins and Conklin 1992), *cannot be expected to support students' focus on learning* over grading. Rubrics that include *descriptions of quality on criteria that reflect learning goals*, however, confer benefits that simple rating scales or point schemes cannot; they *function as the goals toward which students can monitor their progress*" (p. 364; emphasis added).
Brookhart, 2018	46	"The value of a rubric lies in its formative potential (Panadero and Jonsson, 2013), where the same tool that students can use to learn and monitor their learning is then used for grading and final evaluation by instructors. . . . Appropriate criteria are the key to effective rubrics. Trivial or surface-level criteria will not draw learning goals for students as clearly as substantive criteria" (p. 10).

TABLE 2.2: Meta-Analytic Findings on the Effects of Rubrics

Outcome	Number of Studies	Number of Effect Sizes	Effect Size (*g*)
Academic performance	21	54	0.57
Self-regulated learning	5	17	0.23
Self-efficacy	4	4	0.18

Source: Panadero et al, 2023.

As shown in table 2.2, rubrics had a moderate effect on academic performance and smaller (but positive) effects on self-regulated learning and self-efficacy. Panadero and colleagues (2023) cautioned that the small effect sizes for self-regulated learning and self-efficacy should be interpreted in light of the fact that a relatively small number of studies (five for self-regulated learning and four for self-efficacy) were included in the synthesis. Regarding the educational implications of their findings, Panadero and colleagues (2023) commented that "the use of rubrics has a positive influence on students' academic performance" (p. 25). Most interestingly, the meta-analysis also considered *moderator variables*, which are adjacent factors that may impact the effectiveness of an intervention. Based on their analysis of moderator variables for rubrics, Panadero and colleagues (2023) stated:

> It does not seem to matter how many criteria or quality levels the rubrics have, as long as they meet the basic definition of rubrics, and there are no clear indications of rubrics being more or less effective for younger or older students, or for students of different genders. (p. 25)

Taken together, this research indicates that rubrics are an effective means of promoting all students' academic achievement, and educators have a degree of freedom when designing them, as long as they ensure that they include criteria and performance levels.

I should acknowledge here that there are two sides to the rubrics story; not everyone is in favor of their use. In 2020, educational scholars Ernesto Panadero and Anders Jonsson reviewed twenty-seven studies criticizing or arguing against the use of rubrics. They identified three typical themes of these criticisms.

1. Rubrics frequently focus on surface-level details (such as "has five paragraphs") rather than on important criteria (such as "states a compelling thesis") to increase their reliability.

2. Rubrics reinforce systems of scoring, grading, and quantification of student knowledge, which some (such as Kohn, 2006) argue is inappropriate for educational contexts.
3. Rubrics encourage teachers to aggregate information about specific knowledge criteria into overall scores, which is not useful for either feedback or reporting.

If you look carefully at these criticisms, you will see that they all have to do with scoring considerations (reliability, quantification, aggregation). As Susan M. Brookhart (2018) and Panadero and colleagues (2023) highlighted, using rubrics for scoring is optional. Therefore, the approach I present here focuses on the two characteristics found to be most effective—criteria and levels of performance—and leaves scoring as an optional, secondary consideration.

Templates for Learning Progressions

Articulating knowledge items as learning progressions allows students to determine what the next best learning task for them is, based on what they have already learned. This is a core decision during self-regulated learning. Without a progression of performance levels and criteria associated with each performance level, it is not clear to students (1) what they already know about a knowledge item or (2) what the next logical step is to move their learning toward or beyond a knowledge item.

Using the research on rubrics as a guide, the learning progressions I present here include both criteria and performance levels. Performance levels correspond to the previously described performance levels for declarative and procedural knowledge. For declarative knowledge, these are acquisition, organization, analysis, and utilization. For procedural knowledge, they are acquisition, shaping, internalizing, and utilization.

In figures 2.2 (page 36) and 2.3 (page 37), you will see criteria for each performance level in the second column. These generic descriptors delineate what students should be able to do with the knowledge at each performance level. To make these criteria useful, students need to fill in the third column labeled Learning Plan. The questions at each performance level prompt students about what to fill in. Granted, you could fill in the Learning Plan column yourself and give the progression to students, but as you will see in the section on goals in chapter 4 (page 75), it is more effective to teach students to do it. One reason for this is that students' understanding of the knowledge will be enhanced by thinking about what it looks like at each performance level. As Andrade and Heritage (2018) explained:

Declarative Knowledge: *Genres and Text Types*		
	Criteria	**Learning Plan**
Acquisition	Answer questions about facts. Describe vocabulary terms and concepts.	What facts are important? All texts usually have an organizational structure, which varies depending on the genre and text type. The elements of a text are different depending on its genre. Certain genres work best for specific purposes. What vocabulary terms are important? article, biography, caption, characters, conflict, dialogue, drama, fiction, figurative language, glossary, headings, imagery, narrative, nonfiction, plot, poetry, rhyme scheme, setting What concepts are important? genre, structure, purpose, audience
Organization	Draw or describe a structure that organizes the facts, vocabulary terms, and concepts.	What structures could organize the facts, vocabulary terms, and concepts? list, description, classification
Analysis	Describe the relationships among elements of this knowledge. Describe the relationships between this knowledge and related knowledge. Evaluate the claims made about this knowledge. Make and defend claims about this knowledge.	What other knowledge is related to this knowledge? Online genres, such as blogs, webcomics, or social media posts What claims have been made about this knowledge? Different genres set specific expectations for readers regarding content, structure, and style. Genres and text types provide a framework for organizing and categorizing knowledge, making information easier to understand and retrieve. The genre of a text determines the writing style and purpose. What evidence is required to defend claims about this knowledge? Information about how readers respond to elements of different genres Examples of authors using genres for usual purposes Examples of authors using genres for unusual purposes
Utilization	Complete a complex task using this knowledge.	How would this knowledge be used in the real world or in a grown-up job? I am designing a marketing campaign for a new brand of athletic apparel. My job is to design a communication plan that uses the most effective genre and text type for communication with different audiences.

FIGURE 2.2: Sample learning progression for declarative knowledge—Genres and text types.

*Visit **MarzanoResources.com/reproducibles** for a free reproducible version of this figure.*

Procedural Knowledge: *Solving Systems of Linear Equations Using Substitution*		
	Criteria	**Learning Plan**
Acquisition	List the steps or describe the process. Explain when to use the process. Explain why to use the process.	What are the steps involved in performing this process? 1. Solve one equation for one variable. 2. Substitute the expression into the other equation. 3. Solve the new equation for the single variable. 4. Substitute back to find the other variable. 5. Write the solution as an ordered pair. 6. Check the solution. Is the order of the steps important? Yes, the order is important. When is it appropriate to use this process? When one equation is easily or already solved for one variable When the coefficient of one variable is 1 or −1 Why is it advantageous to use this process? Substitution can be more straightforward than elimination, which sometimes requires multiplying both equations by certain factors.
Shaping	Perform the process without errors.	What are common errors made when performing this process? Incorrectly solving for a variable Substituting incorrectly Combining like terms incorrectly Arithmetic mistakes Misinterpreting the solution when there are no solutions or infinitely many solutions How can errors be avoided when performing this process? Double-check algebraic steps when isolating a variable. Use parentheses to keep track of substitutions. Use a calculator. Graph systems of equations to check your work.
Internalizing	Perform the process at the appropriate rate.	Do I need to learn this process to automaticity, or is controlled processing enough? Controlled processing
Utilization	Complete a complex task using this knowledge.	How would this knowledge be used in the real world or in a grown-up job? I am a warehouse manager. My job is to determine the optimal number of units to order of each product to fit within the constraints of space and budget.

FIGURE 2.3: Sample learning progression for procedural knowledge—Solving systems of linear equations using substitution.

Visit ***MarzanoResources.com/reproducibles*** *for a free reproducible version of this figure.*

> Simply being told about goals and criteria is not enough—learners need to intellectually engage with them in order to really get it. . . . When students are meaningfully engaged in co-creating and using rubrics to assess their own work, they tend to learn more, produce higher-quality assignments, and even become better at self-regulated learning. (p. 55)

The two sample learning progressions in this section present examples of how a student might use templates to articulate declarative (figure 2.2) and procedural (figure 2.3) knowledge items as learning progressions.

Figure 2.2 (page 36) shows an example of how a student might complete the declarative knowledge learning progression for the learning topic of genres and text types. If multiple students are working on the same content, they could do this together in a small group. Or, if the whole class is working on the same content, you could lead this as a whole-class activity. But in this example, I use a single middle-school student.

The student begins by answering the Learning Plan questions at the acquisition level. It is highly unlikely that the student will be able to do this from their background knowledge, and if they can, they may need to progress to a different topic, as they likely already have a strong grasp of this one. Instead, the student should use resources to answer the questions. The internet is an excellent resource, especially artificial intelligence (AI) tools like ChatGPT (https://chatgpt.com), Gemini (https://gemini.google.com), Claude (https://claude.ai), and others. The Learning Plan questions make excellent AI prompts. Classroom resources, such as textbooks and other curricular materials, can also provide guidance for students as they answer the Learning Plan questions. A side benefit of this activity is that students preview the content and activate relevant background knowledge. As shown in figure 2.2 (page 36), the student fills in facts, vocabulary terms, and concepts related to genres and text types. As a reminder, vocabulary terms are labels for ideas, and concepts are labels for categories of ideas. Next, at the organization level, the student lists three possible structures that could be used to organize the facts, vocabulary terms, and concepts they listed at the acquisition level. I explain much more about structures and give a list of structures for students to choose from in chapter 3 (figure 3.1, page 55). There is no need for the student to figure out which structure is best (they will do that during organization tasks)—they simply pick several possible structures. At the analysis level, the student fills in knowledge related to the knowledge item at hand. They also search for and select interesting claims related to the knowledge item. The student lists evidence that might be required to defend claims about the knowledge. Finally, the student identifies a real-world task that involves using their understanding of genres and text types.

For a procedural knowledge example, let's use another middle schooler, this time a student who is working on the topic of solving systems of linear equations. In this example, the student is learning to use the substitution method, so they fill in the steps for that strategy at the acquisition level (as shown in figure 2.3, page 37). They also fill in when and why the strategy is used. At the shaping level, the student lists common errors that are made when performing the process and ways to avoid those errors. For the internalizing level, they simply indicate whether this is a strategy that needs to be learned to automaticity, or if controlled processing is enough. Finally, at the utilization level, the student identifies how this knowledge might be used in the real world and describes a complex task that mirrors such use.

For those familiar with the terms *formative* and *summative*, it is likely clear that the learning progressions in figures 2.2 and 2.3 (pages 36 and 37) are primarily built for formative purposes. That is, they are primarily designed to be created by students and used by students to figure out what learning they need to focus on next. However, this does not imply that teachers cannot use them for summative (that is, for scoring or grading) purposes. In fact, it is relatively easy to attach a scoring strategy to this type of learning progression for measurement purposes, making it an effective tool for both measurement and feedback, as I discuss in the next and final section of this chapter.

Measurement and Feedback

You may want to use the learning progressions I described in this chapter for scoring and grading. This is a fairly straightforward process. The first step is to identify the target level of performance for a specific grade level or course and align that with the score that indicates proficiency. Then, you can array the other scores around that target level appropriately.

For example, at the high school level, students learning about the impact of the Cold War on global politics are expected to learn this declarative knowledge to the analysis level, as indicated by a standard such as "Analyze how the Cold War influenced policies in the U.S. and the Soviet Union." Therefore, whatever score indicates proficiency (for example, "proficient") should align with the analysis level of the progression. Whatever score indicates performance above proficiency (for example, "advanced") should align with the utilization level. Scores that indicate that a student has not yet reached proficiency would align with lower levels of the progression. Scores indicating below but approaching proficient (for example, "basic") would align with the organization level, and scores indicating significantly below proficient (for example, "below basic") would align with the acquisition level of the progression.

As another example, consider a middle school standard that requires students to "plan and conduct scientific investigations to answer questions." This procedural knowledge only needs to be learned at the shaping level (without errors); fluency is not required in middle school. Therefore, whatever score indicates proficiency should align with the shaping level of the progression. The score that indicates performance above proficiency would align with the internalizing and utilization levels, and the score that indicates below but approaching proficient performance would align with the acquisition level. The score indicating significantly below proficient would apply to students who have not yet demonstrated acquisition of the process.

Admittedly, there are times when the target level of performance is the acquisition level. This usually only happens in the primary grades, particularly in kindergarten. For example, at the kindergarten level, the target level of performance for learning the letters of the alphabet is the acquisition level, as shown in this Common Core standard for English language arts: "Recognize and name all upper- and lowercase letters of the alphabet" (RF.K.1d; National Governors Association Center for Best Practices & Council of Chief State School Officers, 2010). Therefore, when attaching a scoring strategy to a learning progression for that knowledge, whatever score indicates proficiency ("proficient") should align with the acquisition level, and whatever score indicates performance above proficiency ("advanced") should align with the organization, analysis, and utilization levels. If students have not yet acquired the knowledge, you would assign a score that indicates that ("basic" or "below basic," depending on how far away the student is from the acquisition level).

The self-regulated learning progression presented in this chapter makes both teacher feedback and student self-feedback extremely straightforward. The criteria articulate the goals that students are aiming to meet, and students use the information articulated in the Learning Plan column to facilitate their achievement of those goals. This understanding of current performance and goals creates the soil in which self-regulated learning can flourish. As Andrade and Heritage (2018) wrote:

> When students have a true understanding of the learning goals and criteria, they can do what highly self-regulated learners do: accurately assess their learning as it is developing, and then take action in order to close the gap between their current learning and the goal. (p. 59)

However, the fact that a learning progression facilitates student self-feedback does not mean that teacher feedback is unnecessary. It is essential.

In a 2015 meta-analysis, researchers Steve Graham, Michael Hebert, and Karen R. Harris found that teacher feedback had a significantly higher effect on the learning outcomes of primary and secondary students than self-feedback, peer feedback, and computer feedback, as shown in table 2.3.

TABLE 2.3: Effects of Different Sources of Feedback on K–12 Learning Outcomes

Feedback Source	Effect Size (*d*)
Teacher	0.87
Self	0.62
Peer	0.58
Computer	0.38

Source: Adapted from Graham et al., 2015.

Note that Graham and colleagues' (2015) findings illustrate the general importance of feedback from any source. While smaller than teacher feedback, the effect sizes associated with self-, peer, and computer feedback are not small; these are clearly high-probability strategies for increasing student learning outcomes. However, of all the types of feedback, teacher feedback has the largest effects, according to Graham and colleagues' analysis.

Teacher feedback comes in several flavors. In a 2020 meta-analysis, researchers Benedikt Wisniewski, Klaus Zierer, and John Hattie synthesized 435 studies on feedback (containing 994 effect sizes) involving over sixty-one thousand participants. They found that high-information feedback has the highest effect on student outcomes, as shown in table 2.4 (page 42).

As seen in table 2.4, high-information feedback is significantly more effective than other types of feedback; it not only alerts students to what they need to correct but also prompts them to think about and plan their way forward. Wisniewski and colleagues (2020) elaborated:

> Feedback is more effective the more information it contains. . . . Students highly benefit from feedback when it helps them not only to understand what mistakes they made, but also why they made these mistakes and what they can do to avoid them the next time. (p. 12)

TABLE 2.4: Effects of Different Types of Feedback on Student Learning

Feedback Type	Description	Effect Size (*d*)
High-information feedback	Corrective feedback plus "information on self-regulation from monitoring attention, emotions, or motivation during the learning process" (p. 7).	0.99
Corrective feedback	Gives information "in the form of 'right or wrong' and the provision of the correct answer" (p. 7).	0.46
Reinforcement or punishment	"Pleasant or aversive consequences to increase or decrease the frequency of a desired response or behavior" (p. 7).	0.24

Source: Adapted from Wisniewski et al., 2020.

Others have called high-information feedback by another name: *feedback-feedforward.* This term highlights the effectiveness of feedback that helps students identify the gaps between their current performance and their goal, figure out how to address those gaps, and envision what steps they need to take next to move forward. Andrew J. Martin and colleagues (2022) explained, "Feedback-feedforward provides information to students that can be a basis for adapting their learning via improved self-regulation, better strategies for working on tasks, enhanced understanding, and specific and explicit information about what more needs to be learned or understood" (p. 756).

This kind of "improvement-oriented guidance" (Martin et al., 2022, p. 756) not only models for students the process of self-regulated learning but also provides guidance for them as they practice it. This directly echoes the instructional sequence I presented in chapter 1 (page 7). I finish this chapter by describing how that instructional sequence can be used to teach the knowledge and skills that students need to successfully navigate the knowledge system during self-regulated learning.

Instructional Sequence for Knowledge Skills

If you boil it down to the essentials, this chapter presented procedural knowledge on how to create a learning progression for a knowledge item. This process can be expressed as a learning progression, as shown in figure 2.4. Once the learning progression is articulated, as shown here, it becomes fairly straightforward to use the instructional sequence from chapter 1 (page 7).

Procedural Knowledge: *Articulating a Knowledge Item as a Learning Progression*		
	Criteria	**Learning Plan**
Acquisition	List the steps or describe the process. Explain when to use the process. Explain why to use the process.	What are the steps involved in performing this process? 1. Determine if the knowledge item is declarative or procedural. 2. Select the proper template for the knowledge. 3. Answer the questions in the Learning Plan column using online or print resources. Is the order of the steps important? Yes, the order is important. When is it appropriate to use this process? When you are starting to learn about a new knowledge item Why is it advantageous to use this process? There are two different kinds of knowledge: declarative and procedural. They are learned differently. A learning progression shows what you know now and what you need to work on learning next.
Shaping	Perform the process without errors.	What are common errors made when performing this process? Misidentifying the type of knowledge Not using resources to answer the questions How can errors be avoided when performing this process? Ask yourself if the knowledge includes any kind of process; if it does, it is procedural. Become familiar with resources.
Internalizing	Perform the process at the appropriate rate.	Do I need to learn this process to automaticity, or is controlled processing enough? Automaticity
Utilization	Complete a complex task using this knowledge.	How would this knowledge be used in the real world or in a grown-up job? I am a parent, and my child is sick. I need to learn about their illness and the medical options available for treatment.

FIGURE 2.4: Sample learning progression for articulating a knowledge item as a learning progression.

*Visit **MarzanoResources.com/reproducibles** for a free reproducible version of this figure.*

1. **Explicit instruction:** Present students with the steps of the process for articulating a knowledge item as a learning progression using figure 2.4. Explain when and why to use this strategy.
2. **Modeling:** Think aloud while demonstrating how to articulate a knowledge item as a learning progression using either the declarative or procedural knowledge template.
3. **Practice:** Give students various knowledge items (both declarative and procedural) and ask them to practice expressing them as learning progressions.
4. **Guidance:** Based on their level of success during practice, provide appropriate guidance for each student (as shown in figure 1.2, page 22).

The nature of the practice and guidance you provide should be customized to the level of fluency that you expect students to achieve. If you do not plan to ask students to perform this process independently, then fluency may not be necessary; you might only be aiming for them to learn it at the shaping level. This could be the case if you teach elementary students, or if you only intend to articulate knowledge items as learning progressions in whole-class or guided small-group contexts. However, if you plan to ask students to perform the process independently—as might be the case in a competency-based classroom, where individual students are learning different knowledge items based on their current needs and performance—then you will need to provide enough practice for students to achieve automaticity at the internalizing level.

Here's a hypothetical example to illustrate what this looks like in practice: Ms. Williams teaches ninth-grade biology, and her class is just beginning to study the topic of photosynthesis. Ms. Williams begins by introducing the concept of articulating knowledge items as learning progressions. She projects figure 2.4 (page 43) on the screen and says, "As we begin learning about photosynthesis, we're going to start by articulating this knowledge as a learning progression. This will help us organize what we know and identify what we need to work on next." She then explains how to articulate a knowledge item as a learning progression using the process from figure 2.4.

1. Determine if the knowledge item is declarative or procedural.
2. Select the proper template for the knowledge.
3. Answer the questions in the Learning Plan column using online or print resources.

This is explicit instruction.

Following the process, the class determines that photosynthesis is declarative knowledge, so Ms. Williams switches to a blank version of the declarative knowledge template (figure 2.2, page 36) and writes "Photosynthesis" at the top. Ms. Williams then works with the class to answer the questions in the Learning Plan column about photosynthesis using classroom resources and online tools (such as AI) if answers are not immediately apparent. She switches back to figure 2.4 (page 43) once this is done and asks the class if it was important to do the three steps of the process in order. The class affirms that yes, the order was important. The class then briefly discusses the *when* and *why* questions. This is modeling.

To highlight common errors students might make when articulating learning progressions, Ms. Williams shows them a blank version of figure 2.3 (page 37)—the procedural knowledge template—and asks them to imagine what would happen if they had mistakenly identified photosynthesis as procedural knowledge or tried to answer the Learning Plan questions in figure 2.2 without using resources. Students share that procedural knowledge is things they do, and while photosynthesis is a process, it isn't a process *they* perform—they simply need to learn about it, so it is declarative knowledge. They also share that it would have been really hard to fill in the Learning Plan questions without resources, since they haven't learned about photosynthesis yet.

Ms. Williams presents a short list of other topics in biology and asks students to determine whether each one is declarative or procedural knowledge. If students make errors during this exercise, she asks them to think about whether the knowledge item is something they need to do or something they need to know. This is practice and guidance. In the following weeks and months, as she introduces other units and learning topics, Ms. Williams will ask students to practice filling in the Learning Plan column for those topics, providing appropriate levels of guidance to individual students based on their success. This is also practice and guidance.

To close the lesson, Ms. Williams asks students how useful they think the process of articulating photosynthesis as a learning progression was. Some students recognize that their learning about photosynthesis has already progressed simply by answering the Learning Plan questions. Based on this feedback, the class says it would probably be a good idea to do this process before learning about a topic, and they agree that being able to do it easily and quickly would be useful. Ms. Williams explains that automaticity means they do it without thinking about it, while controlled processing means it is easy and fast, but they still have to think about it. Students agree that it would be great if the process was a habit (automatic), but they'll likely need to think about it quite a bit as they practice it.

Ms. Williams is eager to let students continue learning about photosynthesis, so she briefly asks students how they might use the learning-progression articulation process as adults. One student shares that their father recently had to learn a new coding language, and this process could have helped him with that. Another student shares that their mother's small business recently bought new accounting software, and her employees could have used this process to learn about it.

Summary

Before students can regulate their learning, they must be clear about what the focus of that learning is. What, exactly, are they expected to know and be able to do? In this chapter, we explored the difference between declarative and procedural knowledge and discovered how each type of knowledge is learned. Understanding the distinction between declarative and procedural knowledge is absolutely essential when selecting learning tasks. Trying to practice declarative knowledge is impossible, and analyzing procedural knowledge is usually a waste of time. After acquisition, declarative knowledge needs to be organized and analyzed, and procedural knowledge needs to be shaped and internalized. Proper learning tasks for each kind of knowledge ensure that students can eventually utilize them productively in complex, real-world situations.

As students clarify what they are to learn and plan for that learning, a learning progression can be a very useful tool. When students create the learning progression themselves, it gives them a head start on their learning. Using the research on rubrics, I identified two important characteristics of learning progressions: criteria and performance levels. Students can use the templates in this chapter (figure 2.2, page 36 and figure 2.3, page 37) to analyze knowledge items and articulate them as learning progressions. Once students have articulated knowledge as a learning progression, measurement and feedback become very straightforward: Align your scoring system with the levels of the learning progression for measurement and use the criteria of the learning progression to give students corrective feedback and guidance on their next learning steps.

Once you and your students have a firm grasp on the nature of knowledge and how to properly prepare to learn it, the next step is to give students the skills they need to actually learn it. Happily, this is a straightforward process: The cognitive skills students use to learn knowledge align with the knowledge types (declarative and procedural) and the performance levels (acquisition, organization, analysis, shaping, internalizing, and utilization). In the next chapter, I describe the most effective cognitive skills to use for each performance level of declarative and procedural knowledge.

CHAPTER 3
COGNITION

The word *cognition* is from the Latin word *cognoscere*, which means "coming to know," and that is exactly what cognitive processes do: They allow students to come to know knowledge. Winne (2018) described cognition as an input-output relationship: "Coming to know is a process that takes in information—input—and produces information—output" (p. 36). This fits well with the model of working and long-term memory I presented in chapter 1 (page 7) and the progressions of learning tasks for declarative and procedural knowledge I articulated in chapter 2 (page 25). At each stage of the learning progression, information enters working memory (from the outside world, long-term memory, or both), is processed, and then the result (the output) is encoded in long-term memory.

Interestingly, this input-output conceptualization of human learning originated in the 1950s and 1960s as scientists developed computers that (in some respects) mirrored the information processing model of human thinking. Experimental psychologist Donald E. Broadbent (1958) was particularly responsible for popularizing the idea that human learning and the human brain could be described in terms of "input, internal representation or storage of information, processing, and output" (Wiley & Guerrero, 2023, p. 107). This information processing metaphor is useful when considering the nature of cognitive skills.

Most cognitive scholars agree that cognitive strategies are not specific to any subject. That is, you can use acquisition strategies on declarative knowledge related to English language arts, mathematics, science, social studies, and other school subjects, and the same is true for organization strategies, analysis strategies, and utilization strategies. As long as the knowledge is declarative, the cognitive strategies apply. On the procedural side, the acquisition, shaping, internalizing, and utilization strategies apply to procedural knowledge of all kinds, regardless of subject. As cognitive psychologist Shana K. Carpenter (2023) articulated, "Over 100 years of cognitive science research has revealed specific strategies and techniques that substantially and reliably boost student learning, and that can be readily applied in any course material" (p. 664). To use a term from chapter 1 (page 7), cognitive strategies are *transferable*. Topping (2024) highlighted this aspect of cognitive strategies:

> Long after they have forgotten the detailed knowledge they were taught, the students' refined and widely applicable ability to think should help them perform better in a job or profession and help them solve everyday problems in their personal life, leading to becoming a happier person with a greater sense of well-being. (p. 1)

In summary, students apply cognitive strategies directly to knowledge to learn it. In this book, I present selected cognitive strategies that are used during the declarative and procedural learning tasks shown in figure 2.1 (page 27). Thus, I discuss the following cognitive strategies in this chapter.

- **For acquisition:** Retrieval practice
- **For organization:** Concept mapping and generative learning
- **For analysis:** Examining relationships, evaluating information, and constructing arguments
- **For shaping:** Interleaved practice
- **For internalizing:** Spaced practice
- **For utilization:** Problem solving, decision making, investigation, experimentation, invention, and systems analysis

It is important to recognize that *cognitive strategies are themselves procedural knowledge*. Students acquire, shape, internalize, and utilize cognitive skills. In chapter 4 (page 75), I discuss how metacognitive skills are also procedural knowledge.

Because cognitive strategies are procedural knowledge that students need to learn, I recommend that you ask students to create learning progressions for these strategies, as I described in chapter 2 (page 25). Psychologist Michelle L. Rivers (2021) endorsed this approach, advising teachers to "inform students when and how to study by instructing them on learning strategies and how to use them effectively with the goal of improving learners' . . . procedural knowledge about learning strategies" (p. 846). At the end of this chapter, I explain how cognitive skills can be explicitly taught, modeled, and practiced (with guidance) using the instructional sequence from chapter 1 (page 7).

Cognitive Skills

Cognitive skills allow students to productively interact with knowledge. I would like to give you a definitive list of cognitive skills, but that is impossible. Cognitive skills have been studied by so many different scientists and researchers in so many different fields over the course of hundreds of years that there now exist many and varied lists of cognitive skills, manifestations of cognitive skills, and categories of cognitive skills. As educational psychologist David Moshman (2015) put it, "There is no definitive list" (p. 21). Also, the difference between cognitive processes (acquisition, organization, analysis, shaping, internalizing, and utilization) and their outward manifestations (for example, note-taking, highlighting, diagramming, drawing, rereading, memorizing, searching) adds to the confusion because the outward manifestations of cognitive processes are sometimes ambiguous. For example, as noted by Yingbin Zhang and colleagues (2022), one student might take notes by copying material verbatim from a text or a teacher's notes—a not-so-effective acquisition strategy. Another student might take notes by integrating ideas from several texts and direct instruction to diagram a structure for the information—an effective approach to organization. In a nutshell, cognitive skills can be a bit of a tangled web. To acknowledge this multitude of labels, manifestations, and categorizations, I compiled the information in table 3.1. Take a look at it, but please don't be overwhelmed by it.

TABLE 3.1: Cognition-Related Skills, Activities, and Categorizations

Source	Cognitive Skills
Marzano et al., 1988	**Core thinking skills:** Focusing, gathering information, organizing, and generating **Thinking processes:** Concept formation, problem solving, and research Critical and creative thinking
Gagné et al., 1993	Rehearsal, elaboration, organization
McGuinness, 1999	Sequencing and ordering information, sorting, classifying and grouping, analyzing whole-to-part relationships, comparing and contrasting, making predictions and hypothesizing, drawing conclusions, giving reasons for conclusions, distinguishing fact from opinion, determining bias and checking the reliability

continued →

	of evidence, generating new ideas and brainstorming, relating cause and effect, designing a fair test, defining and clarifying problems, thinking of different solutions, setting up goals and subgoals, testing solutions and evaluating outcomes
Weinstein et al., 2000	Repetition, reorganization, elaboration
Ennis et al., 2005	Induction, deduction, value judgment, observation, credibility, assumptions, meaning
Fischer et al., 2014	Problem identification, questioning, hypothesis generation, construction and redesign of artifacts, evidence generation, evidence evaluation, drawing conclusions, communicating and scrutinizing
Deekens et al., 2018	**Deep strategies:** Coordinating informational sources, making inferences, knowledge elaboration, prior knowledge activation, review, summarization **Surface strategies:** Drawing or diagramming, memorizing, rereading, searching, note-taking
Winne, 2018	Searching, monitoring, assembling, rehearsing, translating
Winn et al., 2019	Elaboration, generation, reflection, spaced retrieval practice, interleaving
Mayer, 2023	**Directed thinking:** Problem solving, reasoning, creative thinking, critical thinking **Nondirected thinking:** Daydreaming, abnormal thinking (as in clinical cases)
Topping, 2024	**Focus and deploy standard thinking processes:** Focus attention, gather relevant information, retrieve and store memories, process information, abstraction, induction **Brainstorm:** Problem definition, concept formation, connected ideas, questioning, assumptions, inferences **Sort ideas:** Analyze, sequence, order, sort, classify and group, logic, deduction, reasoning **Evaluate evidence:** Reflect, assess credibility, give evidence for and against, relate cause and effect, distinguish fact and opinion, speculate **Make conclusions:** Evaluate, judge, interpret multiple criteria, draw conclusions **Propose solutions:** Select responses or actions, solve problems, think of different solutions, think of multiple solutions **Propose additional solutions:** Generate new ideas, creativity, set priorities, set goals

To keep things simple and practical when it comes to cognitive skills, I simply use each performance level in the learning progressions for declarative and procedural knowledge to categorize the cognitive strategies used for tasks at that level. For example, there are specific research-supported strategies that align with how students need to think during acquisition tasks, such as retrieval practice. As another example, there are specific research-supported strategies that align with how students need to think during shaping tasks, such as interleaved practice. Given the plethora of cognitive strategies (as demonstrated in table 3.1, page 49), I focus on those that have a robust research base. The important thing for you and your students to understand when choosing cognitive strategies is that the chosen strategy must match the nature of the knowledge (declarative or procedural) and the desired level of performance (acquisition, organization, analysis, shaping, internalizing, or utilization). Researchers Corinna Schuster, Ferdinand Stebner, Detlev Leutner, and Joachim Wirth (2020) explained, "Cognitive strategies . . . must suit a given learning task" (p. 456). I find it most useful to sort cognitive strategies according to the type of knowledge they act on and the level of performance they induce.

Acquisition

The first level of processing for both declarative and procedural knowledge is acquisition. Acquisition tasks expose students to new knowledge; the goal of an acquisition task is for a student to reproduce or recognize the knowledge they learned at a later time (Wiley & Guerrero, 2023). When students acquire new declarative information, it typically means they are learning vocabulary terms, facts, or concepts related to a topic. When students acquire new procedural information, it usually means they are learning a list of steps in a process or carefully watching someone else perform that process (with the goal of shortly being able to perform it themselves).

One of the most effective strategies to use during acquisition tasks is retrieval practice. *Retrieval practice* refers to any activity that requires a learner to retrieve information from their memory (Carpenter, 2023). For example, after reading a text, a student puts the text away and tries to write down everything they remember from the text. Alternatively, after studying their notes on a topic, a student puts the notes aside and tries to answer a set of teacher-provided practice questions. Or, for a procedural example, after reading a list of steps in a procedure and watching someone else perform the procedure, a student tries to write down the list of steps and draw a series of pictures showing someone performing the process.

Retrieval practice is underpinned by a superabundance of evidence of effectiveness from a variety of contexts and content areas. It has been observed anecdotally since at least the 17th century. Table 3.2 shows selected early observations of the phenomenon.

TABLE 3.2: Early Observations of the Effectiveness of Retrieval Practice

Observer	Year	Description
Francis Bacon, philosopher and scientist	1620	"If you read a piece of text through twenty times, you will not learn it by heart so easily as if you read it ten times while attempting to recite from time to time and consulting the text when your memory fails" (p. 143).
William James, psychologist, philosopher, and scientist	1890	"A curious peculiarity of our memory is that things are impressed better by active than by passive repetition. I mean that in learning (by heart, for example), when we almost know the piece, it pays better to wait and recollect by an effort from within, than to look at the book again. If we recover the words in the former way, we shall probably know them the next time; if in the latter way, we shall very likely need the book once more" (p. 646).
Edward L. Thorndike, psychologist and scientist	1906	"The active recall of a fact from within is, as a rule, better than its impression from without" (p. 123).

In terms of formal research, interest in this highly effective acquisition strategy began in education in the early 20th century (Abbott, 1909; Fitch, Drucker, & Norton, 1951; Gates, 1917; Sones & Stroud, 1940; Spitzer, 1939; Thorndike, 1914) and continued to be refined and deepened into the 21st century (Roediger & Karpicke, 2006a, 2006b). Retrieval practice has been found to be effective with elementary students (Goossens, Camp, Verkoeijen, & Tabbers, 2014; Jaeger, Eisenkraemer, & Stein, 2015; Jones et al., 2016), middle and high school students (Carpenter, Pashler, & Cepeda, 2009; McDermott, Agarwal, D'Antonio, Roediger, & McDaniel, 2014; Roediger, Agarwal, McDaniel, & McDermott, 2011; Rowley & McCrudden, 2020), and university students (Carpenter et al., 2016; Dobson, Perez, & Linderholm, 2017; Ebersbach, Feierabend, & Nazari, 2020; Hopkins, Lyle, Hieb, & Ralston, 2016). There have been six major meta-analyses of retrieval practice since 2014, which are listed in table 3.3.

TABLE 3.3: Meta-Analyses of Research on Retrieval Practice Since 2014

Meta-Analysis	Number of Studies	Number of Effect Sizes	Number of Participants	Average Effect Size
Rowland, 2014	61	159	Not reported	0.50
Adesope et al., 2017	118	272	15,427	0.61
Schwieren et al., 2017	19	72	Not reported	0.56
Pan & Rickard, 2018	67	192	10,382	0.40
Donoghue & Hattie, 2021	242	374	6,033	0.74
Sotola & Crede, 2021	48	52	7,864	0.42

As shown in table 3.3, six different research teams synthesized over five hundred studies involving over one thousand effect sizes and roughly forty thousand participants. Average effect sizes for the use of retrieval practice range from 0.40 to 0.74, meaning that the use of retrieval practice can be expected to result in a 16 to 27 percentile-point gain in student achievement. The mental processes underlying retrieval practice are still being studied, but Carpenter (2023) explained why one theory works so well:

> One reason that retrieval is beneficial is because it reveals the state of our knowledge. That is, it effectively tells us what we know and do not know. Only by trying—and sometimes failing—to retrieve something can we be aware of what we know (information that we can retrieve successfully) and what we do not know (information that we could not retrieve). Such awareness is critical to successful learning because it identifies the information that is not yet learned and needs to be studied more. (p. 665)

In short, retrieval practice is a cognitive strategy worth teaching.

Applications of retrieval practice are varied, and the exact manifestation of retrieval practice is not as important as making sure that the learner has some opportunity to retrieve information that they previously learned. As Carpenter (2023) observed, "The technique is quite robust and can be flexibly adapted in a number of ways" (p. 664). One of the ways that students can use retrieval practice is by attempting to answer questions about the content they just learned. These might be teacher-generated questions, self-generated questions, or AI-generated questions. Kathleen B. McDermott, Pooja K. Agarwal, Laura D'Antonio, Henry L. Roediger, and Mark A. McDaniel (2014) found that a wide variety of question types were effective during retrieval practice, including the following.

- Selected-response questions (including multiple-choice and true-or-false questions)
- Short constructed-response questions (also known as short-answer questions)
- Extended constructed-response questions (also known as essay questions)

Other studies—such as the meta-analysis by psychologists Lukas K. Sotola and Marcus Crede (2021)—found that simply trying to reproduce previously learned information is also effective, as in the examples at the beginning of this section. Regardless of how students prompt retrieval of previously learned information, a critical element of retrieval practice is called *criterion learning* (Badali, Rawson, & Dunlosky, 2023). Criterion learning is when students set a goal to accurately recall a certain amount of information during retrieval practice and keep practicing until they meet that criterion. An elementary student might use retrieval practice to learn the names of all the states in the United States. They might set the criterion score that they need to correctly label all fifty states on a map at least three times before moving on. A middle school student might use retrieval practice to learn the structures of a cell; they could set the criterion score that they need to accurately name all the cell structures twice before moving on. A high school student might use retrieval practice to memorize important mathematical formulas, setting the criterion score that they need to reproduce their list of formulas from memory five times before moving on.

Organization

The second level of processing for declarative knowledge is organization. The strategies associated with organization all involve students figuring out how pieces of information—both new information and information already in their memory—fit together. The goal of organization tasks is for students to form structures that they can store in their long-term memory. In research literature, these structures are called *schemas*. Information must have a structure to pass from working memory to long-term memory (Wiley & Guerrero, 2023). Simple structures include basic lists of information, while more complex structures include sequence structures (like a timeline), descriptive structures (like a bubble diagram), comparison structures (like a Venn diagram), and cause-and-effect structures (like a flow chart). As with cognitive skills themselves, there is no definitive list of possible structures for schemas, but figure 3.1 shows examples of common structures for organizing information.

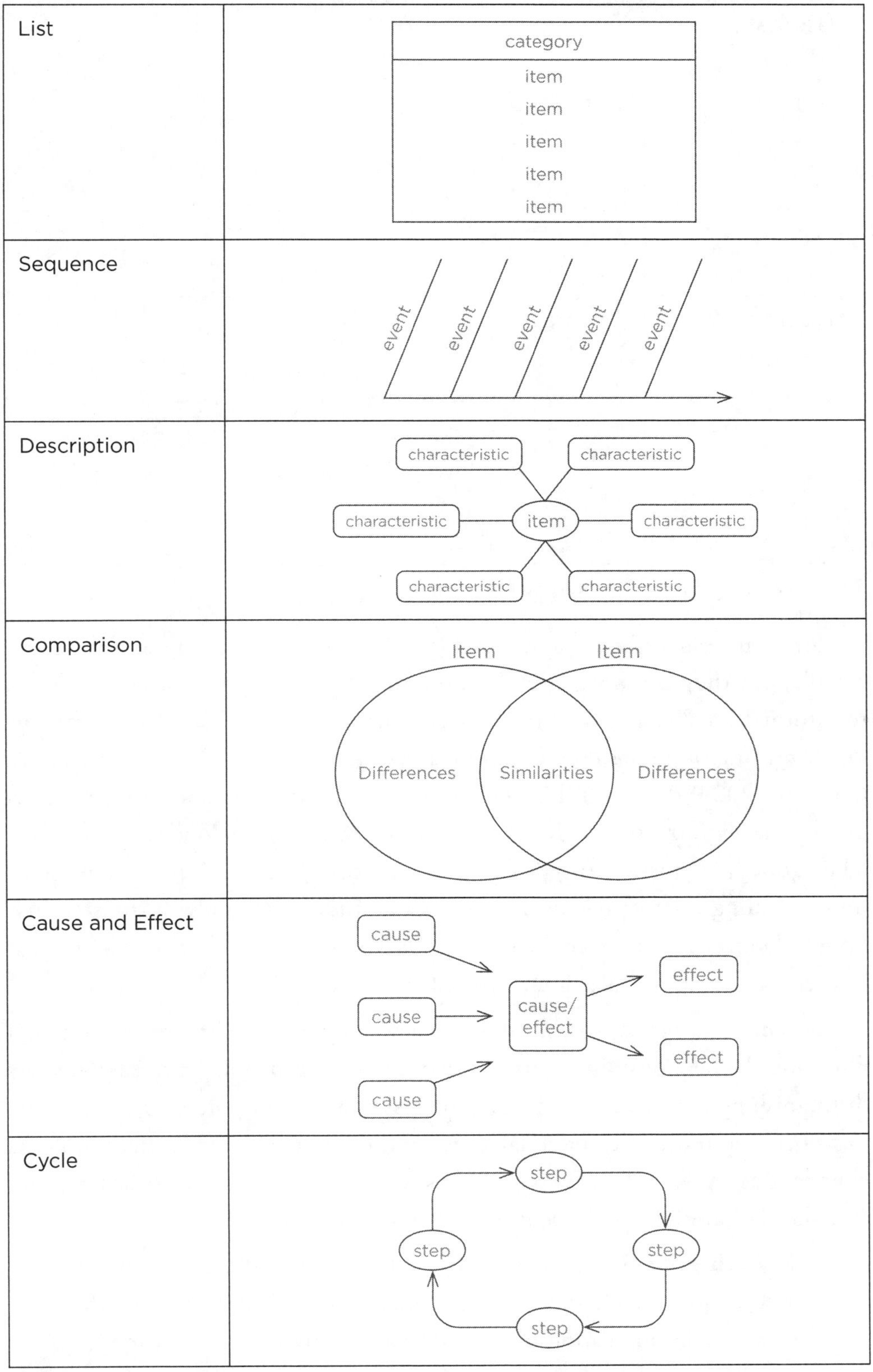

FIGURE 3.1: Examples of structures for organizing and storing information.

continued →

<table>
<tr><td>Classification</td><td>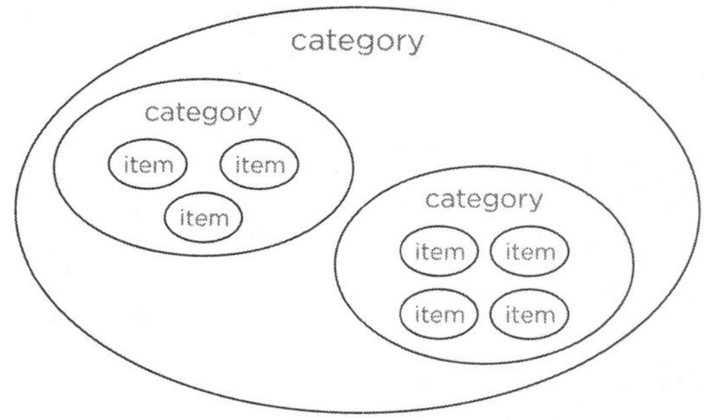
</td></tr>
<tr><td>Argument</td><td>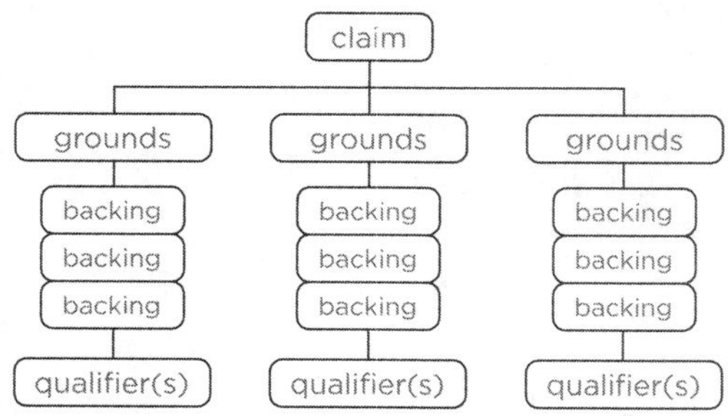
</td></tr>
</table>

Source: © 2022 by Marzano Resources. Used with permission.

Structures might be newly formed if a student is just starting to learn about a topic, but they are more durable and efficient when they involve and attach to information already stored in long-term memory (typically called *background knowledge* or *prior knowledge*). Educational researchers Jennifer Wiley and Tricia A. Guerrero (2023) described this process of schema formation and storage as integrating "new information with relevant prior knowledge from long-term memory." They added, "Constructing this deeper level of representation . . . represents understanding or comprehension, and allows students to apply or transfer their knowledge to new situations" (p. 111). One particularly effective strategy that learners can use to organize information for storage is concept mapping.

In *concept mapping*, students draw or describe a graphical representation that illustrates the relationships among concepts. Concept mapping typically involves distinguishing and labeling individual pieces of information, identifying connections between those informational items, and then drawing or diagramming the connections. As Jonathan St. B. T. Evans (2019) detailed, there are at least four specific relationships that students can identify among informational items.

1. **Exclusion:** Two items are entirely different with no overlap. For example, the physical states of matter—solid, liquid, and gas—have an exclusion relationship; if a substance is in one state, it cannot simultaneously be in another state.

2. **Overlap:** Two items share some (but not all) characteristics. A Venn diagram is commonly used to represent this relationship. For example, cultural elements such as food, language, and festivals overlap with each other; traditions used in festivals might involve both language and food.
3. **Inclusion:** One item is entirely contained by another item. This typically occurs when one informational item is a category label and another informational item fits within that category. For example, quadrilaterals have an inclusion relationship with parallelograms, rectangles, rhombuses, and squares; in turn, there are further inclusion relationships among the subcategories (for example, every square is a rectangle and a rhombus).
4. **Identity:** Two items are the same. This typically occurs when one idea has two different labels that are used, depending on the context. For example, equivalent fractions have an identity relationship; ½ is the same as 2⁄4, 3⁄6, 4⁄8, and so on.

Concept maps can be fairly simple (if students are only working with a small amount of information) or fairly extensive (if students are organizing larger sets of ideas). For example, an elementary student working with declarative knowledge related to the water cycle might use a simple cycle structure to diagram the relationship between evaporation, condensation, precipitation, and collection. In contrast, middle or high school students exploring the causes of a revolution or war might use a combination of interacting structures—such as sequence, description, classification, comparison, and cause and effect—to diagram the complex interacting factors that eventually erupted in a national or global conflict.

Table 3.4 (page 58) presents four meta-analyses of concept mapping conducted since 2018. Notably, the research synthesized here found that simply having students create concept maps is not as effective for learning as having students create concept maps *and explain them* (Eshuis, ter Vrugte, & de Jong, 2022; Kinchin, 2014). In fact, the idea that explaining deepens learning is central to a larger body of work related to organization tasks known as *generative learning theory*.

Generative learning theory posits that when students explain content, either in writing or verbally (Lachner, Ly, & Nückles, 2018), it increases their understanding of the content. A significant body of research supports generative learning's efficacy across contexts and content areas (Adams & Clark, 2014; Ainsworth & Loizou, 2003; Chi, 2021; Chi, Bassok, Lewis, Reimann, & Glaser, 1989; Chi & VanLehn, 1991; De Koning, Tabbers, Rikers, & Paas, 2011; Fiorella & Kuhlmann, 2020;

TABLE 3.4: Meta-Analyses of Concept Mapping

Meta-Analysis	Number of Studies	Number of Effect Sizes	Number of Participants	Average Effect Size
Schroeder et al., 2018	118	142	11,814	0.58
Wong, 2021	30	105	Not reported	0.88
Barta et al., 2022	21	108	1,695	0.53
Anastasiou et al., 2024	55	58	5,364	0.78

Fiorella & Mayer, 2013; Renkl, Stark, Gruber, & Mandl, 1998; Rittle-Johnson & Loehr, 2017; Roscoe, 2014; Wylie & Chi, 2014). Examples of generative activities include composing summaries, drafting explanations, and listing keywords that represent the most important information in a text or information presentation. Generative learning strategies typically require learners to do three things (Fiorella, Stull, Kuhlmann, & Mayer, 2020).

1. Select critical information.
2. Organize critical information into a coherent structure in working memory.
3. Integrate the structure with existing knowledge from long-term memory.

As illustrated by these steps, asking students to explain their concept maps constitutes a generative learning strategy. For example, consider the student who created a concept map for the water cycle using a cycle structure. As the student explains it, they realize that they don't understand how or why water vapor forms clouds during condensation. The student looks for the answer and realizes that there is actually a cause-and-effect relationship in addition to the simple cycle: As the heat that caused evaporation dissipates in the cooler atmosphere, water vapor turns back into liquid water droplets, forming clouds. The student's identification of this additional relationship deepens their understanding of the water cycle; they now understand how heat influences water's state of matter during different phases of the cycle.

Analysis

The third level of processing for declarative knowledge is analysis. When students analyze, they reason about information to identify generalizations and principles; they may also update and revise previously learned knowledge. Analysis strategies often involve examining relationships, evaluating information, and constructing arguments.

Examining relationships differs from the organizational process of identifying relationships in that examining relationships requires students to explicitly identify and then describe, in detail, how different ideas relate to one another. Specifically, based on similarities and differences among ideas, students decide whether and how various ideas are aligned (comparison) or in conflict (contrast) and what metaphorical or analogical relationships exist among ideas. As Wiley and Guerrero (2023) observed, "Presenting alternative representations or contrasting cases to the learner in a way that supports comparison and identification of distinguishing features can help the learner to form generalizations" (p. 112). Activities in which students examine relationships are productive because they lead learners to create generalizations, which is one goal of analysis tasks.

For example, a student studying ecosystems might have identified trophic levels—producers, consumers, and decomposers—as having an inclusive relationship with an ecosystem during organization tasks. As they examine that relationship during the analysis phase, they generate the metaphor "An ecosystem is a community" and explain that the producers (plants) are similar to workers who provide resources and energy, while the consumers (animals) are like community members who use the resources that the producers provide. The decomposers function like clean-up crews, breaking down waste and recycling nutrients. The student observes, though, that consumers are not the only community members who use resources; workers and clean-up crews also eat and use energy. This leads the student to the generalization that energy transfer from one trophic level to the next is not 100 percent efficient. As energy moves through trophic levels in an ecosystem, it diminishes at each step.

Another type of analysis task involves students *evaluating information* to identify and correct errors in their current understanding of information. Educational psychologists Kathryn S. McCarthy and Danielle S. McNamara (2023) explained, "It is impossible to learn new information without encountering false information or incorrectly interpreting information" (p. 214). To move forward with their learning, students need to identify errors or misconceptions in their current knowledge and correct them. For this evaluation to occur, students need to be exposed to a wide range of information about a topic and compare that information with their current knowledge to determine what is accurate. When students learn about a topic from multiple sources, such as those obtained during web searches, coactivation and error identification and resolution are more likely to occur.

For example, a student learning about percentage change thinks that if a growth rate increases from 10 percent to 15 percent, it has increased by 5 percent. During the analysis phase, they watch an online video about percentage change that contrasts absolute change with percentage change. The video shows an example of a population growth scenario for a colony of rats: A starting population of ten rats doubles every three months, leading to a quarterly growth rate of 50 percent. The student realizes that they have confused an absolute change with a percentage change, and if a growth rate increases from 10 percent to 15 percent, it has actually increased by 50 percent, or five percentage points. The student revises their understanding accordingly.

As McCarthy and McNamara (2023) explained, "It is this co-activation of information that drives revision. Having both the correct and incorrect information active in memory at once increases the likelihood that the student will recognize and reconcile the discrepancy" (p. 215). Multiple sources not only lead students to identify and correct errors in their thinking but also acquaint them with the reality that not every source they encounter will be accurate. Many sources are biased or present an argument in favor of a particular position. As students evaluate conflicting sources of information and evidence, they engage in the final type of analysis task: constructing arguments.

Constructing arguments involves making and defending a claim about the knowledge at hand. A claim is simply a generalization about a specific topic, and not every claim merits the construction of an argument. As researchers Chrysi Rapanta and Kalypso Iordanou (2023) explained, claims that merit the construction of an argument meet the following criteria.

- **Related to a problem under consideration:** For example, if a student is studying story elements (characters, setting, plot, conflict, resolution), a claim-meriting argument might be, "People who understand story elements enjoy reading more."
- **Open to discussion:** For example, if a student is learning about the significance of national symbols (flag, anthem, bird, landmarks), a claim-meriting argument might be, "Understanding national symbols makes people more likely to vote."
- **Addressable using information as supporting evidence:** For example, if a student is learning about simple machines, a claim-meriting argument might be, "Levers make it easier to lift heavy objects because they change the direction and amount of force needed."

Issues that merit the construction of an argument might be at the personal level ("Job satisfaction is more important when choosing a career than making money"), at the community level ("We should switch to year-round school"), at the national level ("We should increase funding for renewable-energy research and development"), or at the global level ("Developed countries should increase foreign aid to fight poverty in developing countries"), but in all cases, there should be two or more contrasting perspectives on the issue that can be supported with relevant evidence.

Once learners make a claim, they must evaluate information to determine whether it is credible and accurate before using it as evidence for their claim. Rapanta and Iordanou (2023) explained the connection: "Evaluating available information and its potential use as evidence to support or rebut one's arguments is part of the ability to evaluate information" (p. 580). Learners construct an argument by providing evidence to support the claim that is relevant and sufficient. Multiple pieces of evidence are typically (but not always) required to support a claim. For example, say a student is defending the claim that "learning to solve algebraic equations teaches people how to solve problems in ways that are helpful in other situations." As evidence for this claim, they state, "Breaking down a problem into smaller parts is something you learn when solving algebraic equations that is also useful when solving real-life problems."

In this case, that one piece of evidence could be enough to make an argument. If the student wanted to strengthen their argument, they might add additional evidence, such as the following.

- Finding several different ways to solve a problem is something you learn when solving algebraic equations that is also useful when solving real-life problems.
- Thinking logically is something you learn when solving algebraic equations that is also useful when solving real-life problems.

Once students have articulated their claims and found supporting evidence, the last step is for them to explain why the information they provided as evidence supports the claim; this is the reasoning behind the claim (Omarchevska et al., 2022b). For example, the student could provide reasoning for each of their claims by giving examples of algebraic equations that can be solved using each of the strategies highlighted in their evidence.

- **Breaking down a problem into smaller parts:** To solve $3(2x - 4) + 7 = 19$, you have to do four small steps.
    a. Distribute the 3 to eliminate the parentheses: $(3 \times 2x) - (3 \times 4) + 7 = 19$ becomes $6x - 12 + 7 = 19$.
    b. Combine like terms: $6x - 5 = 19$.
    c. Add 5 to both sides to isolate the variable term: $6x - 5 + 5 = 19 + 5$ becomes $6x = 24$.
    d. Divide both sides by 6 to solve for x: $6x \div 6 = 24 \div 6$ becomes $x = 4$.

- **Finding several different ways to solve a problem:** To solve $2(x - 3) + 4 = 12$, you can use three different methods.
    a. *Distributive property*—Distribute the 2, combine like terms, add 2 to both sides, divide both sides by 2.
    b. *Isolating the variable step by step*—Subtract 4 from both sides, divide both sides by 2, add 3 to both sides.
    c. *Reverse operations*—Undo the addition and subtraction, undo the multiplication, undo the subtraction.
- **Thinking logically:** To solve any algebraic equation, you have to maintain equality on both sides of the equal sign. Therefore, whatever you do to one side, you need to do to the other side.

As seen in these examples, constructing arguments, along with evaluating information and examining relationships, prompts students to identify generalizations and principles related to the knowledge at hand. It also forces them to revisit, clarify, correct, and revise previously learned information. The next step in the declarative knowledge hierarchy of performance levels is utilization; however, utilization is also the top level in the procedural knowledge hierarchy. Therefore, before addressing utilization, let's jump over to procedural knowledge and explore cognitive strategies for shaping and internalizing.

Shaping

During shaping tasks, learners try their hands at executing a process. The goal of shaping tasks is accurate repeated execution of a process. Slow execution is fine (and sometimes desirable) at this stage of practice. One strategy for shaping practice that has a wealth of research supporting it is interleaved practice. *Interleaved practice* involves alternating different types of problems or items while learning. Researchers Jonathan Firth, Ian Rivers, and James Boyle (2021) explained, "Interleaving means varying the order of a set of examples, whereby each item is immediately followed and preceded by an example of a different category/concept rather than appearing in blocks of the same type of item repeatedly" (p. 642). Table 3.5 presents three meta-analyses demonstrating the efficacy of interleaved practice for learning.

Like retrieval practice and concept mapping, interleaved practice has been shown to be effective across contexts and content areas (Carlson & Schneider, 1989; Carlson & Yaure, 1990; Carvalho & Goldstone, 2017; Cross, Schmitt, & Grafton, 2007; de Croock, van Merriënboer, & Paas, 1998; Eglington & Kang, 2017; Guadagnoli & Lee, 2004; Helsdingen, van Gog, & van Merriënboer, 2011;

TABLE 3.5: Meta-Analyses of Interleaved Practice

Meta-Analysis	Number of Studies	Number of Effect Sizes	Number of Participants	Average Effect Size
Chen et al., 2021	67	45	Not reported	0.96*
Donoghue & Hattie, 2021	242	104	972	0.47
Firth et al., 2021	17	32	Not reported	0.65

**Computed from data provided in Chen et al., 2021. Two effect sizes were excluded as outliers.*

Jacoby, 1978; Janssen et al., 2023; Magill & Hall, 1990; Paas & van Merriënboer, 1994; Rohrer & Taylor, 2007; Schneider, Healy, & Bourne, 1998, 2002; Schneider, Healy, Ericsson, & Bourne, 1995; Shea & Morgan, 1979; Simon, 2007). The reason that interleaved practice is effective (and especially more effective than blocked practice, where the same type of problem is practiced over and over) is because alternating different kinds of problems highlights similarities and differences in the problems and the processes used to solve them, giving the learner the opportunity to understand each process more intimately. Additionally, switching between different problem types makes it more likely that students will identify and correct any errors in their execution of each solution process. Wiley and Guerrero (2023) explained:

> Interleaved practice occurs when practice alternates between two or more concepts (such as subtraction and addition) as opposed to the two concepts being practiced separately. Practicing more than one concept at a time allows for comparisons to be made between the concepts. (p. 110)

This type of alternation also forces the learner to identify an appropriate problem-solving strategy for each item (rather than just using the same strategy on all the problems in a practice set, as is possible when all problems in the set are the same type), leading to more effective learning. The following examples highlight how this might manifest in English language arts, mathematics, science, and social studies at the elementary and secondary levels.

- **English Language Arts**
    - *Elementary*—A student might alternate practice on writing simple sentences and identifying parts of speech. This helps them understand how nouns, verbs, and adjectives function within a sentence and improves their overall sentence-construction skills.

- *Secondary*—A student might interleave practice on analyzing themes in literature and writing persuasive essays. By switching between these activities, they can better grasp how to identify central themes in a text and effectively argue their interpretations, improving their analytical and writing skills simultaneously.

- **Mathematics**
  - *Elementary*—A student might practice both addition and subtraction in one session, switching back and forth between the two types of problems. This helps them understand when to use addition versus when to use subtraction and recognize the relationship between these operations.
  - *Secondary*—A student might practice interleaving problems involving quadratic equations and exponential functions. Switching between these problem types helps them understand the distinct approaches required for solving quadratic versus exponential equations and reinforces their ability to select the correct method for each type of problem.
- **Science**
  - *Elementary*—A student might alternate between conducting simple experiments to observe physical changes (like melting ice) and investigating biological processes (like plant growth). This helps them understand different types of scientific observations and the appropriate methods for each.
  - *Secondary*—A student might interleave practice on conducting chemical reactions and analyzing ecological data. By switching between these types of procedures, they gain a broader understanding of experimental design and data interpretation across different scientific contexts, improving their overall research skills.
- **Social Studies**
  - *Elementary*—A student might interleave tasks involving analyzing historical events (such as the American Revolution) and interpreting primary sources (such as letters or diaries from the era). By switching between these activities, they develop a more nuanced understanding of historical context and the skills necessary for historical analysis and interpretation.

- *Secondary*—A student might practice interleaving tasks related to evaluating political systems (such as democracy versus autocracy) and conducting research on international relations (such as trade agreements or diplomatic negotiations). Alternating between these complex topics helps them grasp the broader implications of political systems and develop a more comprehensive understanding of global issues and policies.

Internalizing

Once a learner can perform a process accurately and independently, they should engage in internalizing tasks. The goals of internalizing tasks are speed and the fluent execution of a process. Depending on the process, this fluent execution may manifest as automaticity or controlled processing. Automaticity is the goal for processes that can be automatized (such as solving mathematics facts), and controlled processing is the goal for processes that cannot be automatized (such as the writing process).

One strategy that can be used to develop fluency during internalizing tasks is spaced practice (also known as *distributed practice*). *Spaced practice* involves shorter practice sessions spaced out over time (such as thirty minutes per day for three days) rather than one long practice session (such as ninety minutes on one day). Like retrieval practice, spaced practice was first scientifically investigated around the beginning of the 20th century by German psychologist Hermann Ebbinghaus (1913, originally published 1885). As Carpenter (2023) explained, Ebbinghaus found that "repeated attempts to learn . . . were more effective if they were carried out at different points in time, rather than within the same session" (p. 666). Since then, hundreds of studies have demonstrated similar effects for a variety of content areas across elementary school (for example, Ambridge, Theakston, Lieven, & Tomasello, 2006; Schutte et al., 2015; Seabrook, Brown, & Solity, 2005; Sobel, Cepeda, & Kapler, 2011), middle school (for example, Nazari & Ebersbach, 2019; Randler, Kranich, & Eisele, 2008), and high school (for example, Bloom & Shuell, 1981; Yazdani & Zebrowski, 2006). In 2021, researchers Ouhao Chen, Fred Paas, and John Sweller reviewed forty-eight studies of spaced practice containing forty-five effect sizes. After excluding three outliers, the average effect size for spaced practice was 0.91.

According to Wiley and Guerrero (2023), spaced practice works for the following three reasons.

1. **Spaced practice allows the learner to forget a little bit between practice sessions:** At the next session, the learner must retrieve the

forgotten information from memory. The effort required by this retrieval strengthens the process's salience in memory.

2. **Each practice session during spaced practice is likely to occur in slightly different circumstances than the previous session:** Practicing in a variety of contexts creates more flexibility in a learner's application of the process they are practicing. As Wiley and Guerrero (2023) stated, "With exposure to information in different contexts, the information becomes much more likely to be accessible in different situations and with different cues in the future" (p. 110).
3. **Spaced practice has an advantage because it is harder to focus attention for a long period of time than a shorter period of time:** Practicing something with your full attention for thirty minutes on each of three consecutive days is likely to receive more of your focus than practicing for ninety minutes on one day.

When teaching learners to use spaced practice, it is important to emphasize that the interval between practice sessions needs to be long enough to allow for some forgetting of the process but not so long that students forget the entire process. In her overview of the research on spaced practice, Carpenter (2023) concluded that, when using spaced practice, an appropriate interval between practice sessions is one to two days. The following examples highlight how this might manifest in English language arts, mathematics, science, and social studies at the elementary and secondary levels.

- **English Language Arts**
  - *Elementary*—A student learning to spell new words practices them for ten minutes on Monday and then again for ten minutes on Tuesday, Wednesday, and Thursday.
  - *Secondary*—A student learning to write persuasive essays composes an essay on one topic on Monday, another topic on Tuesday, and a third topic on Wednesday.
- **Mathematics**
  - *Elementary*—A student learning to solve addition problems solves a practice set of twenty problems on Monday and then solves similar sets of problems on Tuesday, Wednesday, and Thursday.
  - *Secondary*—A student learning to solve quadratic equations solves a practice set of ten equations on Monday and then solves similar sets of problems on Tuesday, Wednesday, and Thursday.

- **Science**
  - *Elementary*—A student learning to make observations writes about the development of the class's cress seeds for five minutes on Monday and again for five minutes on Wednesday, Friday, and the following Monday.
  - *Secondary*—A student learning to perform titration practices the process once on Monday, again on Wednesday, and again on Friday.
- **Social Studies**
  - *Elementary*—A student learning to interpret maps answers a series of questions about a map on Monday and then answers different series of questions for different maps on Tuesday, Wednesday, and Thursday.
  - *Secondary*—A student learning to create timelines creates one for the 15th century on Monday, the 16th century on Tuesday, the 17th century on Wednesday, and the 18th century on Thursday.

Utilization

Utilization tasks ask students to use both declarative and procedural knowledge in complex tasks that mirror real-world situations. Robert J. Marzano and Seth D. Abbott (2022) suggested a list of complex tasks:

> - *Decision making* is the process of generating and applying criteria to select between alternatives that appear equal.
> - *Problem solving* is the process of overcoming obstacles or constraints to achieve a goal.
> - *Invention* is the process of creating a new process or product that meets a specific identified need. . . .
> - *Experimental inquiry* is the process of generating a hypothesis about a physical or psychological phenomenon and then testing your hypothesis.
> - *Investigation* is the process of identifying and then resolving differences of opinion or contradictory information about concepts, historical events, or future possible events.
> - *Systems analysis* is the process of describing and analyzing the parts of a system with particular emphasis on the relationships among the parts. (p. 56; emphasis added)

The goal of utilization tasks is not for students to mimic the work of experts; expert performance requires a knowledge base that is acquired over years of study and experience beyond the bounds of K–12 education. Rather, the goal of utilization tasks is for students to learn to engage in the thinking and reasoning processes and tasks that they will use in everyday life. As educational psychologist Clark A. Chinn and learning scientist Ravit Golan Duncan (2021) explained:

> [Education] should enable people to be competent outsiders in science (Feinstein, 2011) and in other fields—that is, people who are not specialists but can reason about information to address issues that they encounter in their lives, from decisions about personal and family health to reasoning about economic policies. (p. 4)

It is also important to remember that learners may justifiably choose to blur the boundaries between various utilization tasks. Many real-life tasks and complex problems do not fit neatly within the bounds of specific complex tasks, such as those listed by Marzano and Abbott (2022). As Moshman (2015) stated, "Such types of thinking cannot be sharply distinguished" (p. 22). Additionally, utilization tasks frequently combine two or more knowledge items, often connecting declarative and procedural knowledge. Therefore, a student might design their own utilization task using a combination of declarative and procedural knowledge and drawing on aspects of several categories of utilization tasks. The following examples highlight how this might manifest in English language arts, mathematics, science, and social studies at the elementary and secondary levels.

- **English Language Arts**
    - *Elementary*—A student combines declarative knowledge of story elements with their procedural knowledge of the writing process to compose a short story.
    - *Secondary*—A student combines declarative knowledge of theme, character development, and plot points with their procedural knowledge about how to write a critical essay to critique a novel.
- **Mathematics**
    - *Elementary*—A student combines declarative knowledge of money with procedural knowledge of addition and subtraction to open a classroom store.
    - *Secondary*—A student combines declarative knowledge of statistics with procedural knowledge of algebra to design a small business model.

- **Science**
  - *Elementary*—A student combines declarative knowledge of plant needs with procedural knowledge of the scientific method to evaluate several sites for a classroom garden.
  - *Secondary*—A student combines declarative knowledge of ecosystems and sustainability with procedural knowledge of investigation to design a prototype for environmentally friendly packaging material.
- **Social Studies**
  - *Elementary*—A student combines declarative knowledge of community services with procedural knowledge about bringing people together to plan a community-service project.
  - *Secondary*—A student combines declarative knowledge about social issues with procedural knowledge about writing persuasive arguments to develop a policy proposal.

Instructional Sequence for Cognitive Skills

As you teach students to use strategies associated with the levels of processing for declarative and procedural knowledge, remember that the strategies themselves are procedural knowledge. Thus, you can use the instructional sequence from chapter 1 (page 7) to teach these processes to students, as illustrated by the example using retrieval practice in chapter 1 (page 21).

I want to acknowledge again that I selected a focused set of cognitive strategies with strong research bases to present in this chapter. Please do not take this to mean that these strategies are the only ones that can be used for each level of performance. They are not. As I explained at the beginning of the chapter (and illustrated in table 3.1, page 49), there are thousands of cognitive strategies available, each with varying amounts of research supporting them.

When selecting strategies to use, I recommend looking for two specific types of strategies. The first type is what I have mainly focused on in this chapter: strategies that are supported by a wealth of research and theory that has accumulated over three or more decades. Strategies such as retrieval practice, interleaved practice, and spaced practice—which have a "long tail" of research—are not guaranteed to work, but they do have a high probability of producing the desired outcomes given the research supporting them. The second type of strategy to consider is what I call a *high-return-on-investment strategy*. These strategies may not have a wealth of research and theory supporting them; in fact, you or a student might have invented the strategy. The key benefits to a high-return-on-investment strategy are that it costs very little to implement (in terms of time, energy, and money) and has the potential to produce significant growth toward the desired outcome. For example, after reading a text, a student might input the text into an AI tool and ask the AI tool to have a conversation with them about it. The investment for this strategy is quite low as long as the student simply copies and pastes the text into the AI tool and spends a reasonable amount of time in conversation with AI. You can find out what the return on this strategy is by using the action-research process I described in the introduction (page 1). If using this strategy leads to more learning than when the strategy is not used, the student may decide to continue using it. It is a high-return-on-investment strategy.

You should also consider the performance level a strategy is designed to induce. Acquisition strategies help students encode information in their memory, organization strategies help students organize information, analysis strategies help students make generalizations about information, shaping strategies help students accurately understand a process, internalizing strategies help students perform a process fluently, and utilization strategies help students use information in complex tasks that mirror real-world functions. The AI conversation strategy in the previous example is an acquisition strategy, designed to help the student store information from the text in memory.

Finally, I recommend that you or your students create a learning progression for each cognitive strategy that students will use. Students need to learn strategies as procedural knowledge before they are expected to use them to learn other content. Figure 3.2 gives an example of a learning progression for the cognitive strategy of retrieval practice.

A learning progression for each strategy structures the student's learning of the strategy and allows you both to track their progress as they learn. Once they've learned the strategy to automaticity or controlled processing, students can use that strategy to learn other content.

Here's what this looks like in practice: Ms. Williams and her class are continuing their unit on photosynthesis. During the next class period, Ms. Williams asks her students to look at the acquisition level of their photosynthesis learning progression, as you can see in figure 3.3 (page 72).

Procedural Knowledge: *Retrieval Practice*		
	Criteria	**Learning Plan**
Acquisition	List the steps or describe the process. Explain when to use the process. Explain why to use the process.	What are the steps involved in performing this process? 1. Identify the new knowledge that you need to acquire. 2. Expose yourself to the new knowledge. 3. Attempt to reproduce the knowledge without using any resources. 4. Use resources to evaluate your reproduction of the knowledge, and identify incorrect or missing elements. 5. Repeat steps 3 and 4 until you are able to reproduce the knowledge accurately and reliably. Is the order of steps important? Yes, the order is important. When is it appropriate to use this process? When acquiring new knowledge Why is it advantageous to use this process? Retrieving knowledge from your memory results in better learning than simply restudying that knowledge.
Shaping	Perform the process without errors.	What are common errors made when performing this process? Using practice questions that don't require you to retrieve the new information Forgetting to check your answers Continuing to retrieve all the information every time rather than just the information you got wrong How can errors be avoided when performing this process? Don't use practice questions; just try to reproduce the information by yourself. Always do step 4 of the process. Set a number of times you need to retrieve something correctly before you stop trying to retrieve it.
Internalizing	Perform the process at the appropriate rate.	Do I need to learn this process to automaticity, or is controlled processing enough? Automaticity
Utilization	Complete a complex task using this knowledge.	How would this knowledge be used in the real world or in a grown-up job? I am the owner of a high-end restaurant. My job is to design a memory system that I can teach to my servers so they can remember customers' orders and requests without writing anything down.

FIGURE 3.2: Sample learning progression for procedural knowledge—Retrieval practice.

*Visit **MarzanoResources.com/reproducibles** for a free reproducible version of this figure.*

Declarative Knowledge: *Photosynthesis*		
	Criteria	**Learning Plan**
Acquisition	Answer questions about facts. Describe vocabulary terms and concepts.	What facts are important? Chloroplasts convert light energy into chemical energy. Energy generated during photosynthesis is stored in glucose molecules. Photosynthesis requires carbon dioxide and water and produces oxygen. What vocabulary terms are important? chloroplast, chlorophyll, stoma, adenosine triphosphate (ATP) What concepts are important? Calvin cycle, light-dependent reactions
Organization	Draw or describe a structure that organizes the facts, vocabulary terms, and concepts.	What structures could organize the facts, vocabulary terms, and concepts? sequence, cause and effect, comparison
Analysis	Describe the relationships among elements of this knowledge. Describe the relationships between this knowledge and related knowledge. Evaluate the claims made about this knowledge. Make and defend claims about this knowledge.	What other knowledge is related to this knowledge? cellular respiration, plant parts, ecology and ecosystems, biochemistry, carbon cycle, climate change What claims have been made about this knowledge? Photosynthesis-like processes may occur in nonphotosynthetic organisms, such as certain animals and fungi. Artificial photosynthesis can be used to produce renewable energy sources, like hydrogen and other fuels. What evidence is required to defend claims about this knowledge? Clarity regarding which characteristics and factors actually constitute true photosynthesis Details regarding the feasibility, efficiency, and scalability of artificial photosynthesis technologies Examples of economically viable uses of artificial photosynthesis Comparisons between the environmental impact of artificial photosynthesis and the impact of other renewable energy sources
Utilization	Complete a complex task using this knowledge.	How would this knowledge be used in the real world or in a grown-up job? I am an agricultural scientist. My job is to optimize the production of a specific crop in a specific region by managing inputs like fertilizers and irrigation in light of the existing sunlight and water availability for the crop.

FIGURE 3.3: Sample learning progression for declarative knowledge—Photosynthesis.

Ms. Williams explains that retrieval practice can help the class learn these facts, vocabulary terms, and concepts and shares figure 3.2 (page 71) with them, highlighting the process for retrieval practice.

1. Identify the new knowledge that you need to acquire.
2. Expose yourself to the new knowledge.
3. Attempt to reproduce the knowledge without using any resources.
4. Use resources to evaluate your reproduction of the knowledge, and identify incorrect or missing elements.
5. Repeat steps 3 and 4 until you are able to reproduce the knowledge accurately and reliably.

She also reviews the other information in the Learning Plan column of figure 3.2. This is explicit instruction.

Then, Ms. Williams uses the retrieval-practice process herself to learn the facts, terms, and concepts in figure 3.3 while thinking aloud. She views a short video with the class in addition to accessing two online texts that provide information. Then, she puts away the resources and attempts to reproduce the information she learned. The class appreciates her transparency; she makes a few errors and acknowledges them during step 4. This is modeling.

She then asks students to engage in retrieval practice for the facts, vocabulary terms, and concepts they need to acquire. As they view videos and read texts, she circulates around the classroom, providing questions, prompts, and tools that students can use as they learn. This is practice and guidance.

In subsequent classes, Ms. Williams teaches her students how to use the cognitive strategies of concept mapping to organize their knowledge of photosynthesis, evaluating information to correct any errors in their knowledge of photosynthesis, and problem solving to engage with real-world problems involving agricultural science. For each cognitive strategy—concept mapping, evaluating information, and problem solving—Ms. Williams constructs a procedural knowledge learning progression and uses it during explicit instruction of that strategy. During later units, she uses the same cognitive strategies and learning progressions to give students further practice and help them develop automaticity with each one.

As students gain more cognitive strategies that they have learned to automaticity, their capacity for self-regulated learning increases, and their need for prompting, guidance, and feedback about those strategies diminishes. Indeed, as Greene (2018) said, “Performance can be degraded when students are asked to consciously enact learning processes for tasks that have been automated" (p. 19). In most self-regulated learning situations, students who have thoroughly learned cognitive strategies will be able to automatically (and sometimes unconsciously) enact acquisition, organization, analysis, shaping, internalizing, and utilization strategies. However, there will always be cases where learning breaks down. When that happens, students need to activate control processes and intentionally select a strategy to address problems with their learning. This intentional monitoring and activation of control processes is commonly referred to as *metacognition* and is the subject of the next chapter.

Summary

Cognitive strategies are critical for self-regulated learning. Students must be fluent with cognitive strategies to learn knowledge. Furthermore, they need to understand that specific strategies work well at specific performance levels for declarative and procedural knowledge. In this chapter, we reviewed strategies for the declarative performance levels (acquisition, organization, analysis, and utilization) and for the procedural performance levels (acquisition, shaping, internalizing, and utilization) that have a solid research base supporting their effectiveness. Retrieval practice, concept mapping, generative learning, examining relationships, evaluating information, constructing arguments, interleaved practice, spaced practice, and complex tasks that mirror real-world situations are all strategies that have a high probability of inducing the processing—and, therefore, the learning—that students need for declarative and procedural knowledge. These cognitive strategies, and others like them, are themselves procedural knowledge and should be taught to students using learning progressions. If you choose to teach students other cognitive strategies, I recommend creating learning progressions for those strategies as well. Once students have learned cognitive strategies for each performance level to automaticity or controlled processing, they will be able to use those cognitive strategies to learn any type of declarative or procedural knowledge. The next chapter, "Metacognition," focuses on how they will manage that learning.

CHAPTER 4

METACOGNITION

Metacognition is the thermostat of self-regulated learning. In the same way that a thermostat continuously monitors the temperature in a room and communicates with heating or cooling systems when needed, metacognition quietly but continuously monitors our thinking. When cognition breaks down, metacognition takes control, turning processes on and off as needed until thinking is repaired and learning can continue (Ackerman & Thompson, 2018). Greater metacognitive knowledge and skill equal more effective regulation. There are two primary functions of metacognition: (1) monitoring and (2) control.

We have all experienced metacognitive monitoring and control. As I described in chapter 1 (page 7), the feeling that something is on the "tip of your tongue"—when you know something but can't retrieve it from memory—happens when cognition breaks down (Hart, 1965, 1967; Winne, 2022). Your working memory is looking for something in your long-term memory but can't find it. Metacognitive monitoring processes detect this failure and begin trying to repair it using control strategies: You try to remember where you were when you last thought about the thing, you try to remember who you were talking to when you last talked about the thing, or you try to remember what you were doing when you learned the thing. If metacognition is successful, you suddenly remember the thing!

As another example of metacognitive monitoring and control, if you are listening to someone talk and suddenly realize that you do not understand what they are saying, cognition has broken down; you cannot make sense of the words you hear (Flavell, 1979; Winne, 2022). Ideally, metacognitive monitoring detects the failure and starts trying to repair it using control strategies: You might ask a question, request that the person repeat themselves, start taking notes, consult a resource, or simply pay closer attention. If metacognition is successful, you are able to figure out what they are saying and follow their subsequent communication.

Table 4.1 reports synthesis studies of the effect of teaching metacognitive skills on academic achievement.

TABLE 4.1: Synthesis Studies of Relationships Between Metacognition and Achievement

Source	Number of Studies	Number of Effect Sizes or Correlations	Number of Participants	Overall Effect on Achievement
Dent & Koenka, 2016	61	490	Not reported	0.41*
de Boer et al., 2018	36	48	Not reported	0.50
Ohtani & Hisasaka, 2018	118	149	369,047	0.58*
Perry et al., 2019	51	Not reported	Not reported	0.65
Muncer et al., 2022	29	74	570,575	0.80*

**Converted to Cohen's* d *from Pearson's correlation* r.

It should be noted that students develop metacognitive skills early in life. As Kuhn (2022) described, a three-year-old child who greets you at the door and says, "I didn't know you were coming!" is making a metacognitive statement (p. 74). However, this is not very sophisticated metacognition, and young children's metacognitive awareness is often flawed. If you are an early childhood or primary teacher and have taught a student the name of something (letters, numbers, objects, people), you've likely witnessed the same student's confident assurance—often moments later—that they "already knew that." Psychologist Kalypso Iordanou (2022) explained that "metacognition develops over the first decades of life," while acknowledging that "our understanding of the trajectories of this development is incomplete, with even adults reported as failing to have good judgments of their own knowing" (p. 402). Nevertheless, there is empirical evidence that even primary students can engage in metacognition to become better at self-regulation through instruction and support (Dignath et al., 2023; Dignath & Büttner, 2008; Hattie, Biggs, & Purdie, 1996; Perry & Rahim, 2011; Roebers, 2017; Whitebread, Bingham, Grau, Pino Pasternak, & Sangster, 2007).

By late elementary school (fourth or fifth grade), students are fully capable of developing sophisticated metacognitive skills, according to research. A 2022 study found that fourth-grade students could learn to improve the accuracy of their metacognitive monitoring judgments and, therefore, choose more effective strategies (metacognitive control) to address learning issues (Oudman, van de Pol, & van Gog, 2022). Ferdinand Stebner and colleagues (2022) found that fifth-grade students were able to learn and apply both cognitive and metacognitive skills to tasks similar to the tasks they were trained in (near transfer) and to tasks quite different from those they were trained in (far transfer). By the beginning of secondary school (sixth grade), students are able to learn and apply all forms of metacognitive monitoring and control (Baars, Wijnia, de Bruin, & Paas, 2020).

In this chapter, I acknowledge that there are many metacognitive skills, strategies, and activities. Since all metacognitive activities occur in pursuit of a goal, I begin by examining how students use metacognitive monitoring and control to pursue their goals. Then, I present three monitoring strategies and three control strategies you can explicitly teach to students. Finally, I end the chapter by sharing an instructional sequence for metacognitive skills.

Metacognitive Skills

As with cognitive strategies, there is no definitive list of metacognitive skills, strategies, or activities. Table 4.2 (page 78) summarizes various lists from various researchers and theorists. As you did with table 3.1 (page 49) in chapter 3, scan the list in table 4.2, but please don't be overwhelmed by it.

As seen in table 4.2, there are many skills, subskills, and strategies that have been identified to be related to metacognition. To simplify the conversation and make this theoretical knowledge base more applicable to K–12 teachers, I group metacognitive skills, strategies, and activities into two categories: (1) monitoring and (2) control. This organizational scheme covers all the skills, strategies, and activities in table 4.2. Beyond that, the cyclical relationship between monitoring and control is the central relationship that governs all metacognitive processes. Monitoring detects problems and issues, and control fixes them. Once control has done its work, monitoring takes over again until it detects a problem, at which point control steps in, and so on. Developmental psychologist Claudia M. Roebers (2017) explained, "There is a constant flow of information between the different components of metacognition" (p. 33), and findings by researchers Victor M. Deekens, Jeffrey A. Greene, and Nikki G. Lobczowski (2018) supported the "interactive and contingent relationship between metacognitive monitoring and control" (p. 75). Perhaps the most straightforward description is this one: "The output of the

TABLE 4.2: Metacognitive Skills, Strategies, and Activities

Source	Metacognitive Skills
Marzano, 1992, 2000, 2007, 2019; Marzano & Arredondo, 1986; Marzano & Heflebower, 2012; Marzano & Kendall, 1996, 1998;Marzano & Kosena, 2022; Marzano & Pickering, 1997; Marzano et al., 1988, 2001, 2017	Goal setting (individual and group) Planning (including identifying steps) Managing conflict Handling controversy Communicating Identifying and acquiring resources Monitoring Evaluating the effectiveness of actions Analyzing perspectives Dealing with feedback Ensuring accuracy Seeking clarity from self and others Setting one's own standards Leveraging creative thinking (divergent and convergent) Sensitivity to one's own and others' interpretations (open-mindedness) Patience (resisting impulsivity) Persistence and perseverance Continuous improvement
Costa & Kallick, 2008, 2009; Kallick & Zmuda, 2017	Persisting Managing impulsivity Listening with understanding and empathy Thinking flexibly Thinking about thinking (metacognition) Striving for accuracy Questioning and posing problems Applying past knowledge to new situations Thinking and communicating with clarity and precision Gathering data through all senses Creating, imagining, innovating Responding with wonderment and awe Taking responsible risks Finding humor Thinking interdependently Remaining open to continuous learning
Roebers, 2017	Monitoring, control
Hoyle & Dent, 2018	Goal setting, planning, self-monitoring, self-control, self-evaluation

Gutierrez de Blume, 2022	**Knowledge of Cognition** Repertoire of cognitive strategies at the learner's disposal Set of heuristics for implementing cognitive strategies Knowing where, when, and why to apply strategies given task demands **Regulation of Cognition** Preparing the ground before a task, such as by identifying resources necessary to complete it and anticipating challenges to be faced Strategies to manage incoming information needed to complete a task Strategies to solve learning difficulties Skills to monitor progress toward task completion Judgment of how well the task was accomplished
Krieger et al., 2022	Goal setting, planning, monitoring goals and progress, reflecting
Kuhn, 2022	False-belief understanding Mentally representing the contents of another's mind Mentally representing and reflecting on the contents of one's own mind Managing one's strategic mental resources in the service of learning Reflecting on one's own thought in the process of reasoning Reflecting on one's own thought in the process of belief revision Epistemological contemplation of the nature of knowing and knowledge more broadly
Muncer et al., 2022	Awareness of one's own strategy knowledge associated with memory and learning Ability to monitor and flexibly control cognitive processing while completing a task Use of cues associated with one's knowledge and skill while progressing through a task
Omarchevska et al., 2022a	Monitoring, regulation
Stebner et al., 2022	Knowledge about learning strategies that directly impact information processing Strategies for planning, monitoring, evaluating, and regulating cognitive processes
Syal & Nietfeld, 2022	Planning, monitoring, evaluating
van der Graaf et al., 2022	Orientating, planning, monitoring, evaluating

continued →

Source	Metacognitive Skills
Winne, 2022	Examine learning actions, appraise effects of learning tactics, plan adaptations to current method for learning
Zhang et al., 2022	Goal setting, planning, self-monitoring, control, evaluating
de Ruig et al., 2023	Task orientation, goal setting, planning, self-evaluating, monitoring, organizing
Hoch et al., 2023	Monitoring (tracking, reviewing, assessing) and control (decision making, taking action)
Li et al., 2023	Goal setting, reflecting
Xu et al., 2023	Planning, monitoring, reflecting
Veerman, n.d.	Orientation, goal setting, planning, monitoring, checking, evaluation, recapitulation

metacognitive monitoring function provides the input to the metacognitive control function" (Fiedler, Ackerman, & Scarampi, 2019, p. 89). Before we explore strategies for monitoring and control, we need to take a closer look at goals, given their critical role in both monitoring and control processes.

Goals

From a student's perspective, monitoring means asking, "How am I doing?" Control means using the answer to the monitoring question to determine, "What do I need to start, stop, or keep doing?" As highlighted by these questions, goals are a central and critical aspect of both monitoring and control. Answering the monitoring question ("How am I doing?") requires some sort of criterion or standard (a goal) that the student can use to measure their current performance: "How am I doing *in relation to* my goal?" And the control question is also governed by the goal: "What do I need to start, stop, or keep doing *to get closer to* my goal?" Researchers Gregory Arief D. Liem and Corwin Senko (2022) explained, "Goals serve as a standard against which the current state is compared, and the resulting discrepancy generates a force that gives rise to goal-directed actions" (p. 2168). Essentially, goals are targets. If you'd like a scholarly definition of *goal,* here are two.

1. "A *goal* is a mental representation of what one is attempting to attain" (Schunk & DiBenedetto, 2020, p. 2).
2. "A *goal* is a cognitive representation of desired or undesired future states that directs motivated behavior" (Liem & Senko, 2022, p. 2168; emphasis added).

I began chapter 1 (page 7) by talking about goals because the goal's the thing that holds all the aspects of self-regulated learning together. As Winne (2022) said, "Without goals, learners have no basis for rationally selecting any particular option about what to learn and how to learn it" (p. 778). All goals are not created equal; research indicates that goals are most effective when they are appropriately difficult, appropriately specific, appropriately proximal, and appropriately referenced (Locke & Latham, 2002, 2013; Martin et al., 2022; Schunk & DiBenedetto, 2020).

- *Difficulty* is learner specific; ideal goals match or slightly exceed a previous personal best (Martin et al., 2022).
- *Specificity* limits the number of pathways that can be used to reach a goal; fewer pathways mean fewer opportunities to get sidetracked (Inzlicht et al., 2021).
- *Proximity* sets a deadline for a goal that is days or weeks away rather than months or years; if you get off track, an imminent deadline prompts you to quickly re-evaluate your plan and make a new plan to get on track (Kim, Yu, Wolters, & Anderman, 2023).
- *Reference* involves who or what you compare your performance to; the most adaptive goals compare performance to an external criterion (like a rubric or learning progression) or one's own previous performance (Urdan & Kaplan, 2020).

There is a wealth of research supporting each of these characteristics of goals. (See Simms, 2024, for a review of goal-related research.) The approach to creating learning progressions that I described in chapter 2 (page 25) is designed to take each of these characteristics into account. In terms of *difficulty*, a learning progression allows students to identify their current level of performance for a particular knowledge item. Once they know where they are at, they can aim to meet or exceed that level of performance, resulting in appropriately difficult goals. In terms of *specificity*, creating a learning progression narrows the number of pathways to a goal by articulating an ordered set of tasks to reach the goal. *Proximity* is facilitated by the multiple levels of a learning progression; students might aim to move up one performance level every few days or weeks. And relative to *reference*, a learning progression exists independent of anyone else's performance; the student is not aiming to beat another student's performance but rather simply trying to move forward on the learning progression.

In summary, learning progressions, like the ones I introduced in chapter 2, allow students to set growth goals. *Growth goals* involve a student articulating how much they want to grow rather than what they want to achieve. This means that a growth goal, by definition, is self-referenced: "They are typically operationalized as personal best (PB) goals and self-based goals" (Martin et al., 2022, p. 753). Research has found that growth goals are associated with increases in academic aspirations and academic engagement—both of which are themselves positively associated with academic achievement (Burns, Martin, & Collie, 2018; Martin et al., 2022).

One reason for these positive associations is that growth goals involve a high level of clarity. Martin and colleagues (2022) explained, "With growth goal setting, the effort or performance needed to outperform a previous best is specifically known (as opposed to trying to beat others, whose performance is often unknown until the task is finished; Martin 2006)" (p. 755). Another reason for the efficacy of growth goals is that they highlight the gap between a student's current state and their desired state and articulate steps to help students close that gap. This gap constitutes "a dissonance that students are motivated to resolve" (Martin et al., 2022, p. 755), and clearly articulated steps help make the gap a solvable problem. To help students set growth goals, you can use the following process.

1. Ask a student to articulate (or provide them with) a learning progression for a specific knowledge item.
2. Ask the student to identify their current level of performance relative to the learning progression.
3. Ask the student how many performance levels they think they can advance to in a specified amount of time (ideally a few days to a few weeks).
4. Have the student write down their growth goal and revisit the goal periodically as they work toward it.
    - If the student achieves their goal early, continue to step 5 as soon as they achieve it—don't wait for the remaining time to run out.
    - If the student is not progressing toward their goal at a rate that will allow them to achieve it, work with them to identify what additional support or effort they need to add to achieve their goal.
5. When the student achieves their goal, celebrate!
6. Ask the student to set a new goal, either for the same learning progression (in which case, return to step 3) or for a different learning progression (in which case, return to step 1).

Before we finish our discussion of goals, let's discuss goal re-evaluation. While a bit counterintuitive, this capacity can be a productive skill for students to possess.

As researchers Yeo-eun Kim, Shirley L. Yu, Christopher A. Wolters, and Eric M. Anderman (2023) explained:

> Disengaging from a goal, either temporarily or entirely, can be an important strategy to improve subjective well-being and save personal resources. . . . When goals are unrealistic or entail excessive costs, disengaging from a desired outcome and replenishing resources has been closely associated with well-being across the lifespan. (pp. 81, 82)

During the COVID-19 pandemic, a study found that the ability to abandon unproductive goals and re-engage with alternative goals led to lower stress, fewer depressive symptoms, and better life satisfaction (Hamm, Tan, Barlow, Delaney, & Duggan, 2022). Usher and Schunk (2018) endorsed goal re-evaluation as well:

> Although it may be unpopular to say, one key to success is knowing when to give up. As a general rule, learners should be encouraged to put forth effort to pursue their goals, but at some point efforts might be counterproductive to their ultimate aims. (p. 32)

In the classroom, goal re-evaluation can take several forms, depending on the context and constraints of your school and a student's grade level and learning profile. For example, an elementary student who is not progressing toward their goal at the internalizing level for the topic of multiplication facts might decide to take a break from that goal and focus instead on measuring time intervals. After a mental rest and the opportunity to focus on other learning, the student returns to their multiplication-facts goal to attempt it again. At the middle school level, a student who is struggling to achieve analysis-level goals in social studies might put those goals on hold and set an alternative goal for achieving controlled processing with the cognitive strategy of constructing arguments. After honing their skill with arguments, they are better equipped to work toward their analysis goals in social studies. At the high school level, a student might be enrolled in an Advanced Placement class but be struggling to stay engaged with the content. While you are conferencing with the student, you realize that this student is not really interested in the content of the class, nor is the content relevant to their career aspirations and plans. You might (in collaboration with the student's parents and other staff members) counsel the student to abandon their goal of learning this course content and instead spend their learning time on a topic that is more interesting to them and directly relevant to their long-term goals and plans.

Once students have set goals and made plans to track their progress toward those goals (re-evaluating them as necessary), they are ready to engage in metacognitive monitoring and control. Here, I present six strategies—three for monitoring and three for control—that, like the strategies in chapter 3 (page 47), have a strong research base supporting them.

Monitoring

Metacognitive monitoring involves asking specific questions about one's performance and progress toward a goal. These questions can address both cognition and motivation. In this chapter, I focus on the monitoring of cognition, and in the next chapter, I cover motivation. As would be expected given the general research on the effects of teaching metacognitive skills, studies have demonstrated the positive effects that teaching monitoring skills has on academic performance. In a meta-analysis, Dignath and colleagues (2023) found that monitoring interventions increased academic achievement, with an effect size of d = 0.42. Other meta-analyses have found similar effect sizes.

- Self-assessment (a type of monitoring) interventions improved academic achievement for K–12 students, with an effect size of d = 0.40 (Brown & Harris, 2013).
- Self-grading (a type of monitoring) interventions improved achievement, with an effect size of g = 0.34 (Sanchez, Atkinson, Koenka, Moshontz, & Cooper, 2017).
- Self-monitoring improved achievement, with an effect size of d = 0.47 (Guzman, Goldberg, & Swanson, 2018).
- Self-assessment interventions improved achievement, with an effect size of g = 0.45 (Yan, Wang, Boud, & Lao, 2023).

Even very young students can engage in monitoring. Researchers Marie Geurten and Christine Bastin (2019) observed metacognitive monitoring skills in two- and three-year-olds, and a 2011 study found that students' metacognitive monitoring improves during preschool and kindergarten (Lyons & Ghetti, 2011). By age six, students will spend more time looking at content that they think they haven't learned yet (a monitoring judgment; Destan, Hembacher, Ghetti, & Roebers, 2014). By age eight, students will go back and look at content that they think they haven't learned as well as other content (also a monitoring judgment; van Loon, de Bruin, Leppink, & Roebers, 2017).

Nevertheless, young students' monitoring judgments are typically overoptimistic (de Bruin, Kok, Lobbestael, & de Grip, 2017; Roebers & Spiess, 2017); they think they know more than they actually know. The quality of metacognitive monitoring begins to improve during the elementary years (Schneider & Löffler, 2016), but accurate monitoring judgments are an ongoing battle. Children, adolescents, and adults consistently overestimate what they know, are overconfident in their judgments, and overoptimistically predict how well they will do on assessments (Destan & Roebers, 2015; Oudman et al., 2022; Rutherford, 2017; Szpunar, Jing, & Schacter, 2014). This is unfortunate because, if students think they have already learned something, they are unlikely to expend any more time and effort on it.

Moreover, there seems to be a correlation between performance and judgment accuracy. Students with lower performance typically overestimate their performance, while students with higher performance typically underestimate their performance (Ackerman & Thompson, 2017, 2018). Overestimating one's knowledge of content usually results in not spending any more time learning it. When a student, in reality, does not know the content, this decision is misguided and will result in poorer outcomes, creating a doubly unfortunate situation for already low-performing students. As Sophie Oudman, Janneke van de Pol, and Tamara van Gog (2022) explained:

> Overestimating one's learning is problematic because one could terminate practicing and move on to another task before the initial skill has been mastered and therefore additional practice or instruction would be needed to fully master the initial skill. Thus, this finding that low performing students overestimate their performances more than high-performing students is even more problematic because making appropriate choices about subsequent learning activities is arguably even more important for low-performing students as they are furthest away from mastering the learning goals. (p. 216)

To productively control their learning, students must be able to "accurately judge their own learning" (Omarchevska et al., 2022a, p. 1028). Thus, it benefits all students, especially low-performing students, to teach metacognitive monitoring skills and provide metacognitive monitoring tools.

Before we explore monitoring strategies, here's some good news! Research indicates that one of the best strategies for increasing students' metacognitive monitoring judgments is to explicitly teach them cognitive strategies, which I addressed in chapter 3 (page 47). Educational scholar Antonio P. Gutierrez de Blume's 2022 meta-analysis of interventions for improving metacognitive monitoring found that "individuals exposed to some form of learning strategy instruction exhibit enhanced metacognitive monitoring accuracy regarding their learning" (p. 693) and that "explicit strategy instruction has been shown to decrease . . . overconfidence" (p. 684). Therefore, if you are using the instructional sequence from chapter 1 (page 7) to teach the cognitive strategies (or others like them) from chapter 3 (page 47), you are already on your way to teaching students to accurately monitor their metacognition and learning.

Evaluate Cues

Accurate metacognitive monitoring is not an innate human skill. As I noted previously, learners of all ages tend to deceive themselves (usually in the direction of overconfidence) about what they know and how well they know it. As Carpenter (2023) stated, "Accurate awareness of one's own knowledge does not occur naturally" (p. 665). Therefore, an important step in improving students' metacognition (and overall self-regulated learning) is to teach students to evaluate the cues they are using to make judgments about their learning.

Inaccurate monitoring judgments are fairly easily explained: When students use reliable data sources to assess their learning, their judgments are better. When students use unreliable data sources to assess their learning, their judgments are worse. According to a 2023 study, students do not directly observe or sense what is happening in their memory: "Judgments of learning are not based on an observation of one's memory strength" (Weissgerber & Rummer, 2023, p. 2). Similarly, Klaus Fiedler, Rakefet Ackerman, and Chiara Scarampi (2019) explained, "People cannot directly 'read' their knowledge and the quality of their own cognitive processing, but instead, must base their judgments on cues experienced when they perform the task and immediately after stopping performing it" (p. 93). Students gather data about their memory and learning from various sources and then use that information to infer how well they have learned something: "Judgments of learning are inferentially derived from various cues" (Weissgerber & Rummer, 2023, p. 2). Like other data sources, the cues that drive monitoring judgments can be reliable or unreliable.

Cues are hints or clues about what is happening in a student's brain relative to their learning. There are lots of different kinds of cues; table 4.3 describes several. The important thing to remember about cues is that they are not always reliable. Some cues have *high diagnosticity*: They help students make accurate monitoring judgments. But other cues have *low diagnosticity*: They mislead students about their learning. As Wang and Lajoie (2023) explained, "Monitoring accuracy is affected by the diagnosticity of cues learners have utilized to make metacognitive judgments" (p. 8). Therefore, in addition to listing common cues used to make monitoring judgments, table 4.3 also indicates how each cue can potentially mislead learners to make inaccurate judgments about their learning.

TABLE 4.3: Types of Cues

Cue	Description	Example	How It Can Be Misleading
Fluency	Ease and speed in processing information or performing a task	Short texts Large fonts Processes with few steps Helpful formatting (bullets, headings)	Learners overestimate their understanding of easy-to-process information and tasks that are relatively easy to perform.
Familiarity	Sense of prior exposure to information or a task	Use of your name or peers' names Conversational language	Learners overestimate their understanding of knowledge that feels familiar.
Time	How much time has been spent learning content	Long study sessions Reading long texts Long classroom units	Learners overestimate their understanding of knowledge they have spent more time learning.
Accessibility	How easily knowledge can be retrieved from memory	Compelling visuals Memorable characters Engaging presentations	Learners overestimate their understanding of knowledge that is easy to remember.
Consistency	Alignment of new knowledge with previously learned knowledge or experiences	Generalizations that reinforce one's beliefs Conclusions that align with one's experiences	Learners overestimate their understanding of knowledge that aligns with their prior knowledge or beliefs.

Source: Ackerman & Thompson, 2018; Baars et al., 2020; de Bruin et al., 2020; Fiedler et al., 2019; Hoch et al., 2023; Schnaubert et al., 2021; Wang & Lajoie, 2023.

To teach students to evaluate cues, provide the following questionnaire (figure 4.1) and have them answer the questions.

1. **Assessment:** How close are you to demonstrating the performance level you are working on? ☐ Beginning ☐ Halfway ☐ Almost ☐ Done
2. **Evidence:** If you checked off *beginning* or *halfway*, keep working! If you checked off *almost* or *done*, why do you think so?
3. **Evaluation:** Was your response to question 2 similar to any of the following? ☐ This was pretty easy to learn. ☐ I already knew most of this. ☐ I worked on this for a long time. ☐ I can remember a lot of this. ☐ This all makes sense to me.
4. **Confirmation:** If yes, ask your teacher for their assessment of your learning.
5. **Re-evaluation:** If your teacher's assessment is different from yours, keep working on this level until your assessments agree.

FIGURE 4.1: Evaluating cues questionnaire.

Visit ***MarzanoResources.com/reproducibles*** *for a free reproducible version of this figure.*

For example, let's say a student is working on dividing fractions at the shaping level of performance. During assessment, they rate themself as *done*, since they think they are ready to move on to the internalizing level. As evidence, they say, "My dad is an accountant, so I'm really good at math." As they evaluate the cues they are using, they notice that their response is based on familiarity—they feel comfortable with mathematics. So, they ask their teacher for confirmation. The teacher asks the student to solve a series of ten practice problems and draws their attention to an error in their process: They often forget to find the reciprocal of the divisor fraction before multiplying. The teacher rates the student's demonstration as *halfway*. Given the discrepancy between their teacher's assessment and their own, the student makes a plan to keep practicing at the shaping level.

Use Tools

Another strategy to help students improve the quality of their monitoring is to provide them with metacognitive monitoring tools. These typically take the form of questions or prompts and can be used with all K–12 students. In support of this, the meta-analysis by Dignath and colleagues (2023) of monitoring interventions examined the effectiveness of monitoring tools on various age groups and found that "monitoring tools seem to work for all. . . . Monitoring tools are equally effective for [fostering self-regulated learning] and achievement among learners of all age groups" (p. 37). Other research has articulated the characteristics of effective monitoring tools (Chang & Brainerd, 2022; Dignath et al., 2023; Martin et al., 2022; Nückles, Roelle, Glogger-Frey, Waldeyer, & Renkl, 2020; Rhodes, 2019; Rhodes & Tauber, 2011; Scheiter, Ackerman, & Hoogerheide, 2020; Siedlecka, Paulewicz, & Wierzchoń, 2016; Travers, Morisano, & Locke, 2015). Table 4.4 synthesizes that research into a list of research-based characteristics of effective metacognitive monitoring tools. The second column gives examples of questions and prompts that exemplify these characteristics. These are in the first person because I recommend that students ask themselves these questions, but you could also ask students these questions in the third person. The third column articulates nonexamples of each characteristic that should be avoided.

TABLE 4.4: Characteristics of Effective Monitoring Questions and Prompts

Characteristic	Examples	Nonexamples
Addresses the content that is being learned rather than students' learning behaviors	What are some examples of the knowledge I am learning? What are some situations in which I could use the knowledge I am learning?	What learning tools did I use today?
Addresses the learner's understanding of the content rather than their perception of the content	Which important ideas do I understand? Which important ideas do I still not understand?	What was difficult about my learning today? What was easy about my learning today?
Addresses metacognition rather than cognition	What strategies are working best to help me understand the knowledge?	What did I already know? What did I learn? What do I want to know more about?

continued →

Characteristic	Examples	Nonexamples
Provides feedback about learners' monitoring judgments	[To the teacher] Do you agree with my judgment of my learning? Do you think there are other strategies that will help me learn this knowledge?	Am I done learning yet?
Makes learners responsible for implementing feedback	Based on my teacher's feedback, what knowledge am I going to learn next? Based on my teacher's feedback, what strategy will I use to learn that knowledge?	The next thing I'm going to learn is . . . To learn that, I'm going to . . .
Guides the learner toward important metacognitive functions	How much progress have I made toward my goal for this knowledge? What strategies worked well with this particular knowledge?	I should make an entry in my reflective journal.
Prompts the use of a specific metacognitive strategy	What are my plans for learning this knowledge? What parts of this knowledge will I learn before I pause to reflect?	What will I do to monitor my learning today?
Identifies aspects of support that were helpful	What support was most helpful to me while learning this knowledge?	What support or help do I need from the teacher?
Delays judgments of learning	What level of performance for this knowledge do I think I achieved a few days ago?	How do I think I did with my learning today?

Source: Chang & Brainerd, 2022; Dignath et al., 2023; Martin et al., 2022; Nückles et al., 2020; Rhodes, 2019; Rhodes & Tauber, 2011; Scheiter et al., 2020; Siedlecka et al., 2016; Travers et al., 2015.

The first row of table 4.4 articulates one of the most important characteristics of metacognitive monitoring tools: They focus students on their learning behaviors *in the context of the specific content they are learning*. According to Dignath and colleagues' (2023) meta-analysis, "studies that used tools focusing on both—monitoring of the learning content and of the learning behavior—produced significantly higher effects on achievement than studies that used a tool stimulating monitoring of the learning behavior" (p. 33). Thus, notice that all the examples in the second column of table 4.4 reference ideas or the knowledge in some way.

The overall aim of metacognitive monitoring tools is to help students focus on cues, offering greater potential to produce accurate monitoring judgments. The form that these tools take (reflection opportunities, journals, and so on) is quite flexible. Students can ask themselves these questions formally or informally, you can ask them as questions (in the third person), or you can rephrase them as hints (for example, "Think about what strategy you just used that led you to understand this content"). You can ask students to write down their responses, share their responses verbally, or visualize their responses. As researchers Erdem Onan, Wisnu Wiradhany, Felicitas Biwer, Eva M. Janssen, and Anique B. H. de Bruin (2022) explained:

> Metacognitive prompts refer to facilitative tools (e.g., questions, hints, and visualizations) that help students to monitor their learning and reflect upon their task experiences (Bannert, 2006). Previous studies have shown that metacognitive prompts can increase students' access to diagnostic indicators (or "cues") about their current state of knowledge. (p. 2452)

One way to supercharge the efficacy of formal opportunities for metacognitive monitoring—such as when you ask all students in a class to respond to a series of questions or prompts in a journal—is to precede individual monitoring with a group discussion. A 2022 study investigated ways to improve students' reflection and found that "introducing a classroom discussion before answering reflection prompts was found to be an effective add-on. . . . The effects of classroom discussion are stronger for students with lower academic abilities compared to average and above-average students" (Eshuis et al., 2022, p. 710). Strategies such as this scaffold the reflection experience for students and support those who may need it with metacognitive monitoring.

Critique Learning

Self-assessment can support both cognitive strategies and metacognitive monitoring. In fact, in a 2017 meta-analysis, researchers Ernesto Panadero, Anders Jonsson, and Juan Botella found that self-assessment was a necessary condition to reap many of the benefits of rubrics (such as the learning progression I presented in chapter 2, page 25). They commented, "Self-assessment is thought to contribute to student learning by, for instance, enhancing the clarity of the learning goals, involving students in monitoring the learning process, and facilitating reflection about the final product or learning outcome" (p. 76). Interestingly, student self-assessment has been found to align fairly well with teachers' assessment judgments: Carmen E. Sanchez, Kayla M. Atkinson, Alison C. Koenka, Hannah Moshontz, and Harris Cooper (2017) computed correlations between primary and secondary students' self-reported grades and the grades assigned to them by teachers and found a correlation of $r = 0.67$. Correlations closer to 1.00 indicate a higher degree of alignment, while correlations closer to 0.00 indicate a lower degree of alignment.

However, student self-assessment is not the same thing as student self-reported grades. Andrade and Heritage (2018) explained that *self-assessment* is "a formative process during which students reflect on the quality of their learning, judge the degree to which it reflects explicitly stated goals or criteria, and revise accordingly" (p. 88). In its simplest form, self-assessment involves identifying the level of performance that one's own product or demonstration meets. A more complex manifestation of self-assessment might involve analyzing one's own product or performance to identify areas of strength and opportunities for growth (Panadero, Brown, & Strijbos, 2016). Andrade and Heritage (2018) proposed three key steps for self-assessment.

1. Understanding learning goals and criteria
2. Critiquing learning in terms of goals and criteria
3. Revising ideas or work

The learning progressions I introduced in chapter 2 (see figure 2.2, page 36, and figure 2.3, page 37) address step 1 of this process by clearly defining the levels of performance and criteria for a declarative or procedural knowledge item. Step 2—critiquing learning in terms of goals and criteria—involves monitoring.

There are plenty of ways that students can gather data to help them critique their learning in terms of the goals and criteria articulated in the learning progression. At the acquisition level, students can write out lists of information or processes from memory or answer questions about facts, vocabulary terms, and concepts. At the organization level, students' concept maps and written explanations serve as data, and at the analysis level, students' comparisons, metaphors, analogies, generalizations, and arguments provide evidence of their learning. At the shaping level, accurate execution of a process might be captured through a practice set of problems or footage of students performing a process. Topping (2024) reported that video footage of students executing procedural knowledge "was often added to self-assessment in various ways to improve accuracy" (p. 86). For internalizing practice, accuracy and speed are the two data points that matter most, and for utilization tasks, students can evaluate their use of decision making, problem solving, invention, experimentation, investigation, and systems analysis to complete their tasks.

Once students have gathered data, the criteria on the learning progression guide their critiques of their learning. If a student's data demonstrate that the student has met the criteria for the level they are working on, they should move on to the next level. If not, they should keep working at their current level, aiming to improve their learning to meet the criteria and gathering data as evidence of that learning. For example, consider a student who is working at the analysis level for the topic of literary themes in English language arts. The student has created a series of metaphors and analogies that examine the relationships between how heroism is depicted in Homer's *Odyssey* and J. K. Rowling's *Harry Potter* series. Consider the following metaphors.

- ***The Odyssey* and *Harry Potter* books are two symphonies composed in distinct eras.** Just as each symphony has its own unique melody, rhythm, and instruments, each story of heroism offers a different tune to the theme of bravery. *The Odyssey* is like a classical symphony with grand, epic movements and heroic feats, while *Harry Potter* is like a modern symphony with a contemporary beat and magical harmonies. Both convey the essence of heroism, but through different styles and contexts.
- **Heroism is a majestic, ancient oak tree in *The Odyssey* and a vibrant, contemporary bonsai in *Harry Potter*.** The oak tree, representing *The Odyssey*, stands tall and enduring, with its broad branches and deep roots symbolizing the classical, heroic journey filled with grand quests and timeless struggles. The bonsai, representing *Harry Potter*, is carefully cultivated and intricate, embodying the modern, nuanced approach to heroism where personal growth and magical challenges shape the narrative. Both trees are remarkable in their own right, showcasing different yet equally impressive forms of strength and resilience.

Consider the following analogies.

- ***The Odyssey* is to *Harry Potter* what a traditional tapestry is to a modern graphic novel.** *The Odyssey* is like a tapestry woven with intricate, detailed scenes from ancient mythology, representing a rich and complex narrative with deep cultural significance. On the other hand, *Harry Potter* is like a graphic novel that offers a vibrant and dynamic story through visually engaging illustrations and contemporary language, reflecting modern storytelling techniques and themes. Both present captivating stories, but their methods and styles reflect their different historical and cultural contexts.

- **The depiction of heroism in *The Odyssey* is to a traditional knight's quest in medieval lore what the depiction of heroism in *Harry Potter* is to a modern superhero's adventure in a comic book.** In *The Odyssey*, Odysseus's heroism involves epic battles, divine interventions, and a quest that spans vast geographical and mythical landscapes, much like a knight's valorous deeds in ancient tales. In contrast, Harry Potter's heroism involves overcoming personal challenges, mastering magical skills, and facing contemporary moral dilemmas, similar to how a superhero navigates modern challenges with special powers and personal growth. Both portray heroism, but their approaches reflect the cultural and temporal contexts of their respective stories.

The student compares this evidence to the criteria articulated in the learning progression for this topic.

- Describe the relationships among elements of this knowledge.
- Describe the relationships between this knowledge and related knowledge.
- Evaluate the claims made about this knowledge.
- Make and defend claims about this knowledge.

The student decides that their evidence meets the first two criteria but recognizes that they have not yet evaluated claims or constructed arguments about literary themes. They decide to work on that next.

As I noted previously, there were three steps in Andrade and Heritage's (2018) self-assessment process. The learning progressions in chapter 2 (page 25) address step 1 (understanding learning goals and criteria), and the strategy in this section for gathering and evaluating data against the criteria in the learning progressions addresses step 2 (critiquing learning in terms of goals and criteria). Step 3 (revising ideas or work) is the job of metacognitive control, which I discuss next.

Control

Metacognitive control involves making decisions and taking action to improve one's own learning. I addressed metacognitive monitoring first in this chapter because monitoring judgments drive metacognitive control decisions. A student's judgment about how well they learned knowledge heavily influences their decisions to dedicate more time and effort to that knowledge and on which strategies to use to keep learning. As Wang and Lajoie (2023) explained, "Metacognitive control processes are informed by metacognitive judgments students make about learning" (p. 9).

Accurate monitoring leads to better control decisions. Table 4.5 provides additional evidence for this claim.

TABLE 4.5: Accurate Monitoring Leads to Better Control Decisions

Source	Evidence
Rawson & Dunlosky, 2013	"A student who accurately evaluates his or her own learning progress will be able to isolate just those materials that require further practice" (p. 71).
Ackerman & Thompson, 2018	"Conclusions that reasoners draw are determined, at least in part, by whether they are content with their initial answer or whether they search for an alternative. Thus, monitoring and control processes are key for understanding why and when reasoners are content with their initial representations, and the conditions that lead them to expend the necessary effort to supplement it" (p. 3).
Kubik et al., 2022	"Miscalibrated metacognitive monitoring results in ineffective control" (p. 376).
Syal & Nietfeld, 2022	"Overconfident learners may prematurely end their learning because they believe that they have adequately mastered the learning material" (p. 2).
Vuorre & Metcalfe, 2022	"Metacognitive monitoring and knowledge, when accurate, may be used to select appropriate items for further study or to seek assistance to improve comprehension" (p. 270).
Wang & Lajoie, 2023	"Monitoring accuracy may influence the effectiveness of subsequent metacognitive control" (p. 8).
Wiley & Guerrero, 2023	"The ultimate value of supporting better monitoring accuracy among learners is that it then can help them to make effective decisions of what to re-study as they attempt to master material on their own" (p. 114).

Some of the most important control decisions that students make during self-regulated learning have to do with strategy selection. Students frequently choose ineffective cognitive strategies when they are engaged in self-regulated learning (Baars et al., 2017, 2020; de Bruin, Roelle, Carpenter, & Baars, 2020; Janssen et al., 2023; Wang & Lajoie, 2023). This is largely due to the misconception that more difficult cognitive strategies produce less learning. When students have to work hard to learn something, they often underestimate their learning. Conversely, as we discussed in our examination of misleading cues, when students experience ease or fluency while learning, they often overestimate their learning.

This confusion can lead students to choose learning strategies that are easier but less productive. As Eva M. Janssen and colleagues (2023) explained:

> Both students' judgments of how well they are learning with a specific strategy as well as their inclination to use that strategy are affected by their experiences during studying (Kornell & Bjork, 2007; Soderstrom & Bjork, 2015). However, these experiences are not necessarily predictive of actual learning outcomes. For instance, students often misinterpret feelings of fluency during studying . . . as an indication of learning. (p. 4)

Research shows that difficult or challenging cognitive strategies frequently produce more and better learning. Researchers often refer to these challenges as *desirable difficulties*. Convincing students to use cognitive strategies that involve desirable difficulties is doubly hard because not only are effective cognitive strategies typically difficult to enact, but the greater and better learning they produce is sometimes not immediately evident. As researchers Anique B. H. de Bruin, Julian Roelle, Shana K. Carpenter, and Martine Baars (2020) explained:

> Regulating effort is particularly challenging because typically there is a non-linear relation between invested effort and achieved learning outcomes. In the case of learning conditions that create "desirable difficulties," this challenge is even greater, because these learning conditions cost high effort, do not show an immediate learning benefit, but lead to higher learning and more transfer at a delay. (p. 907)

Consider three effective cognitive strategies I described in chapter 3 (page 47): retrieval practice, interleaved practice, and spaced practice. Each of these has an easier, less effective alternative strategy. It is easier to reread notes or a text than to test your recall of the information. It is easier to solve a set of similar problems that all require the same strategy than to solve a set of varied problems where you must identify the strategy each one requires. It is easier to do all your practice at one time than to schedule multiple shorter practice sessions over several days. Despite the unequivocal research results supporting the use of the more difficult strategies, students don't use them (Foster, Rawson, & Dunlosky, 2018; Yeo & Fazio, 2019). Carpenter (2023) elaborated:

> Why do students avoid retrieval and spacing? Research suggests that these tendencies could arise from students' beliefs about the effectiveness of these techniques. More specifically, retrieval and spacing require effort. It is harder to try to retrieve something from

> memory than to simply read it again, and it is harder to retrieve something that was seen two days ago compared to something that was just seen a moment ago.
>
> The fact that retrieval and spacing involve effort has been confirmed through studies in which students are asked to use these techniques and then report how much mental effort was involved. In these studies, students rate retrieval as more effortful than study (Foster et al., 2018; Hanham et al., 2017; van Gog et al., 2011), and they also rate spacing as more effortful than massing. (p. 668)

Cognitive scientists Skylar J. Laursen and Chris M. Fiacconi (2022) offered another example:

> Consider for example a student who needs to study for upcoming tests in two different subjects. Naturally, the student may consider one of the two subjects "easier" than the other. If the student were to interleave their study of the more difficult subject with the easier one, the way in which they utilize effort cues (e.g., study time) to monitor their learning of the difficult material may change in comparison to if this material was studied separately and on its own. Although previous research has demonstrated a benefit in retrieval when interleaving, as compared to massing study (Brunmair & Richter, 2019; Guzman-Munoz, 2017), the results of the current research suggest that this highly endorsed practice could potentially affect the accuracy with which students evaluate their learning. (p. 28)

In summary, strategies that involve desirable difficulties are better for learning but require more effort, and students are unlikely to use them unless they realize and remember this. Onan and colleagues (2022) wrote:

> Many students . . . make poor learning strategy decisions (Blasiman et al., 2017), such that they avoid effortful but effective strategies—the so-called desirable difficulties (Bjork, 1994)—in favor of less effortful but less effective strategies (e.g., highlighting text). (p. 2452)

And Winne (2018) commented:

> A prime example is distributed practice [another name for spaced practice] where the schedule for reviewing previously studied content spreads out over a timeline rather than reviewing immediately after or very close in time to a first study session. Laboring to recall

> prior material that is not "at hand" enhances memory for that content (e.g., Roediger & Butler, 2011). But learners prefer material to be blocked or massed, setting a stage for overconfident judgments of retrievability because material they study repeatedly in one session is recognized rather than having to be retrieved. Recognizing material is easier but less productive. (p. 43)

And the worst of it is, students don't always recognize an effective cognitive strategy when they see (or experience) one. A 2016 study found that only 33 percent of the students in the study thought blocked practice was better than interleaved practice, despite the fact that 60 percent of them performed better after engaging in interleaved practice (Yan, Bjork, & Bjork, 2016). Researchers Afton Kirk-Johnson, Brian M. Galla, and Scott H. Fraundorf (2019) and Onan and colleagues (2022) found similar results: Students preferred blocked practice even after experiencing the greater efficacy of interleaved practice. So, what do we do about this?

Recognize Desirable Difficulties

One of the simplest ways to correct students' misconceptions about cognitive strategies that involve desirable difficulties is to simply tell them that effortful strategies (such as retrieval practice, interleaved practice, spaced practice, and so on) are more effective than their counterparts (restudy, blocked practice, massed practice). In their study of students' perceptions of interleaved practice, Onan and colleagues (2022) found that students did not avoid effortful strategies due to laziness. Rather, they avoided effortful strategies because they believed they were less effective than easier strategies:

> Students did not avoid interleaved practice because they wanted to minimize their effort investment. Instead, students were misled by their inaccurate monitoring of effort and learning and avoided interleaved practice because they think the higher effort does not lead to more learning. (Onan et al., 2022, p. 2473)

Onan and colleagues (2022) found that, once they were aware of their misconceptions about desirable difficulties, "students were willing to *embrace the effort* induced by interleaved practice. . . . They recognized that their effort paid off in terms of learning gains" (p. 2473). In many cases, setting students' expectations regarding desirable difficulties may be enough to help them overcome their misconceptions and use more effortful but effective strategies.

However, simply telling students may not be enough. Therefore, I also recommend incentivizing the use of cognitive strategies. This does not necessarily mean offering rewards to students who use effective cognitive strategies, although you could try that; neuroscience research strongly supports the use of rewards (Anderson, 2016a, 2016b; Milner, MacLean, & Giesbrecht, 2023), and some cognitive psychologists concur (Hidi, 2016). Instead, Rivers (2021) recommended making effortful but effective cognitive strategies a regular part of classroom instruction. For example, if you are teaching students to use retrieval practice, model practice testing during class. Make sets of questions available to students and either require or reward them for completing practice tests. Make low-stakes quizzes a daily occurrence in the classroom. As I explained in chapter 1 (page 7), these activities should be accompanied by explicit instruction to students about what retrieval practice is, when they should use it, why they should use it, and how they should use it.

An additional benefit of frequently incorporating effective cognitive strategies into classroom activities is that the more students use them, the more they develop the habit of using them. As Kuhn (2022) explained, students' strategy preferences do not change immediately but rather shift slowly over time:

> The shift from use of a weaker strategy to a more effective one, numerous studies have now shown, does not occur abruptly at a single point in time (Chinn, 2006). Rather, a range of strategies coexist in an individual's repertory over an extended period and are drawn on variably, with only a gradual shift toward less frequent application of weak strategies and more regular use of stronger ones, with the stronger gradually dominating the weaker and becoming the consistent approach. This pattern has been shown across a wide range of ages, populations, and problem types. . . . Some of the strategies in a learner's repertory eventually win out over others not simply by chance or because they are more mentally available but because they are better—that is, more powerful. (p. 75)

For a list of all the cognitive strategies from chapter 3 (page 47), along with suggestions for incorporating them into regular classroom practice, see the appendix (page 131).

As students use these strategies over and over again in the classroom, they will gradually develop the habit of using them to learn, which—according to Kuhn (2022), Logan Fiorella (2020), and others—is powerful enough to overcome their misconceptions that more difficult strategies are less effective. Another way to help students choose effective strategies is to teach them to consciously inhibit their use of less effective strategies—an idea I discuss next.

Practice Inhibition

Inhibition is the ability to suppress "a dominant response in favor of a subdominant response" (Spiegel, Goodrich, Morris, Osborne, & Lonigan, 2021, p. 331). Rick H. Hoyle and Amy L. Dent (2018) described it as the ability to "deliberately override a dominant, automatic, or proponent response" (p. 54). The importance of inhibition is often acknowledged in lists of metacognitive skills as "resisting impulsivity" or similar phrasing, but it actually serves many functions in metacognition (Diamond, 2016; Kuhn, 2022), including the following.

- Focuses attention by suppressing distractions in the environment
- Promotes responsible interaction by suppressing inappropriate motor or verbal actions
- Allows delayed gratification by suppressing impulses for immediate action
- Facilitates perspective taking by temporarily suppressing one's own perspective (known as *bracketing*; also, see Stanovich, 2016)
- Improves well-being by suppressing unhealthy choices
- Enhances decisions by suppressing task-irrelevant options
- Refines metacognitive monitoring by suppressing overconfidence

Relative to metacognitive control, an important use of inhibition is to suppress students' selection of less effective strategies in favor of more effective, though effortful, strategies. As Kuhn (2022) stated, metacognitive control "must not only select an effective strategy but equally if not more important, it must inhibit the selection of inferior strategies" (p. 76). Even very young students can benefit from improving their inhibitory control. Sonja Kälin and Claudia M. Roebers (2022) found that "children became more accurate and faster in their responses from kindergarten to 2nd grade . . . [and] showed substantial improvements in their monitoring accuracy compared to kindergarten" (p. 1089). These gains can be interpreted to have resulted from the development of students' inhibitory control (Diamond, 2013).

At a basic level, improving inhibition involves practicing starting, stopping, and waiting behaviors. A 2019 study found that, for young students, adding new rules to familiar games (such as adding new colors and corresponding actions to Red Light, Green Light) improved students' inhibitory control (McClelland et al., 2019). For example, in addition to green light (walk forward), yellow light (walk slowly), and red light (stop walking), purple light (jump forward), blue light (turn in a circle), and orange light (sit down) were also used. For older students, inhibitory control practice could involve prompting them to wait before responding to a question, making a decision, or (as previously suggested) judging how well they understand knowledge or how much background knowledge they already have about a topic (Ackerman & Thompson, 2018). For example, if you are using a student-response app in class (an excellent way to incorporate retrieval practice), disable any features that incentivize students to respond quickly. Instead, adjust the settings so that students are forced to wait ten seconds before responding. After students submit their answers to the question, informally poll the class to find out who changed their answer during that time and whether their accuracy improved as a function of waiting.

One of the most important functions of inhibition occurs when students encounter a perspective that differs from their own. This happens formally when students evaluate information and construct arguments, but also informally when they have conflicts with other students, teachers, friends, or family members. In both formal and informal cases, students' ability to metacognitively *bracket*—or set to the side—their perspectives and beliefs is critical to their ability to perceive and understand the perspectives and beliefs of another person (Diana, 2020; Gergen, 2015; Kuhn, 2019, 2020, 2022; Kuhn & Modrek, 2018; Leslie, 1987; Macagno, 2016; Macagno & Walton, 2018; Moshman, 2015; Stanovich, 2016; Stanovich & West, 1997; Walton, 2007). During bracketing, one's own perspective does not cease to exist or cease to be relevant. As Kuhn (2022) explained:

> One cannot compare dual representations (of own and other mind) unless one has distinguished them. Doing so thus entails representing one's own perspective as an object of cognition, clearly a metacognitive task, as a basis for the crucial task of constructing a representation of the other's perspective. (p. 77)

I like to think of metacognitive bracketing as taking my own perspective and putting it in a mental box, which I then set to the side. My attention is then available to fully listen to and seek to understand the perspective of another person; while I listen, I fill up a different mental box. Once I perceive that both boxes are full (that is, that both perspectives are fully articulated), I can compare the two boxes, metacognitively standing outside of them and comparing them.

To enable students to practice this manifestation of inhibitory control, present a topic on which students will likely have a variety of perspectives and beliefs (for example, climate change). Once you have introduced the topic, ask students to articulate their perspectives and beliefs about the topic, either by writing them down or recording them; it is important to capture their perspectives in some form of media that is outside of their heads. Next, students physically pick up the paper or device on which they recorded their perspectives and place it somewhere outside of their immediate workspace. Then, present several perspectives on the topic at hand and ask students to pick one that is different from their own and articulate it (either in writing or in a recording). Finally, have students bring their own perspectives back to their workspace, and engage them in a comparison activity to identify similarities and differences between their perspective and the alternative perspective they selected.

Focus on One Task

The final metacognitive control behavior I will address involves students' ability to focus their attention, particularly when they are faced with distractions. Temptations to *multitask*—to work on multiple tasks "at the same time"—abound, especially temptations toward media multitasking, or multitasking with digital devices (Kong, Meng, Deng, Wang, & Sun, 2023).

The term *multitasking* itself is a misnomer, as doing two tasks simultaneously is only possible when one of the tasks is truly automatic (such as running on a treadmill or riding a stationary bike; Dönmez & Akbulut, 2021). Typically, what we call multitasking is, in fact, *divided attention* between two tasks—that is, alternating our attention between one task and the other (Kaminske, Brown, Aylward, & Haller, 2022). Because this sort of *task switching* has high cognitive costs, multitasking is extremely inefficient (Mark, Czerwinski, & Iqbal, 2018; Mitchell, Harman, Lee, & Lee, 2008; Ophir, Nass, & Wagner, 2009; Orhan, Castellano, Khelladi, Marinelli, & Monge, 2021; Puranik, Koopman, & Vough, 2020) and impairs performance in significant ways. In particular, task switching negatively impacts:

- Students' performance (Giunchiglia, Zeni, Gobbi, Bignotti, & Bison, 2018; Junco & Cotten, 2012)
- Students' ability to remember information (Uncapher & Wagner, 2018)
- Students' well-being (Brooks, 2015)

Media multitasking is the most prevalent form of multitasking among students (Popławska, Szumowska, & Kuś, 2021; Segijn, Voorveld, Vandeberg, Pennekamp, & Smit, 2017; Zhou & Deng, 2023); about 30 percent of students have a smartphone by age nine. By age thirteen, that rises to 70 percent, and 90 percent of students aged fourteen and older have a smartphone (Rideout, Peebles, Mann, & Robb, 2022). *Media multitasking*, according to a 2015 article, involves "simultaneously engaging in two or more types of media or using media while engaging in non-media activities" (van der Schuur, Baumgartner, Sumter, & Valkenburg, 2015, p. 206).

When students are learning, they are likely facing the temptation to multitask with media. Metacognitive control allows them to successfully resist that temptation, and it is worth resisting. Media multitasking impairs learning, self-regulation, and well-being, as illustrated by the research findings listed in table 4.6.

TABLE 4.6: Media Multitasking Impairs Learning, Self-Regulation, and Well-Being

Source	Research Findings
van der Schuur et al., 2015	"The weight of evidence appears to support a . . . *negative relationship* between media multitasking and the three domains of youths' functioning [*cognitive control, academic performance*, and *socioemotional functioning*]" (p. 213, emphasis added).
Cain et al., 2016	"Greater media multitasking correlated with *worse statewide standardized test scores measuring academic achievement in math and English*. . . . We found a link between greater media multitasking and *worse academic outcomes in adolescents*" (pp. 1938, 1940, emphasis added).
Beuckels et al., 2021	"Various kinds of media multitasking behaviors in class, such as text messaging (Clayson and Haley, 2013), social media usage (Lau, 2017), mobile phone usage (Kuznekoff and Titsworth, 2013), and laptop usage (Fried, 2008; Sana et al., 2013; Gaudreau et al., 2014), have been demonstrated to be related to *poor learning performances, lower course grades, and performance on tests*" (p. 10, emphasis added).
Wiradhany & Koerts, 2021	"Frequent media multitasking had . . . significant associations with a *decrease of attention regulation* (z =.16), *lower levels of inhibition/higher levels of impulsiveness* (z =.22), an *increase of memory problems* (z =.16), and a *decreased behavior regulation* (z =.19). . . . We found that heavy media multitasking was associated with *higher frequency of mind-wandering, higher distractibility, and more problems with task switching*" (p. 290, emphasis added).

In their 2023 meta-analysis, researchers Fanchang Kong, Sujie Meng, Huiying Deng, Meiru Wang, and Xiaojun Sun summarized forty-three studies involving 118 effect sizes and 5,194 participants, finding a:

> negative association [d = −0.23] between media multitasking and global cognitive control. Our finding was consistent with prior empirical studies (e.g., Baumgartner et al., 2014; Ophir et al., 2009). This relationship indicated that heavy media multitasking might be an effective predictor for damaging individuals' cognitive control abilities. (p. 21)

Multitasking, and media multitasking in particular, threatens students' success in school and in life. Therefore, I recommend that you teach students strategies to avoid multitasking.

First, students should view temptations to multitask as alternative goals competing for their attention. If they are aware that alternative goals are present in a learning situation, they are better able to address the conflict and make more informed—and hopefully more effective—choices about which goals to pursue. As Kim and colleagues (2023) explained:

> New and/or existing (but lower priority) goals can be activated during the goal pursuit for various reasons including boredom, text messages or phone calls from friends, and tasks taking longer than expected. Students can try to be consciously aware and notice if another goal starts to impact or interfere with one's pursuit of the target goal. By carefully monitoring the surrounding environment and the activation of alternative goals, students can be more equipped to deal with potential conflicts. (p. 78)

For example, if a student is engaged in a learning task but receives frequent notifications from social media apps on their phone, they should recognize these notifications as competing goals that can distract them from their primary goal of learning. By consciously acknowledging that checking their phone is an alternative goal that might interfere with their focus, the student can make a more deliberate choice to either turn off notifications or set specific times to check their messages, thus helping them stay on track with their learning.

Second, students who struggle with choosing to multitask instead of staying focused on their learning can create implementation intentions. According to Kim and colleagues (2023), *implementation intentions* are "detailed plans where individuals commit to respond to particular situational cues and outline how to implement the planned behaviors (e.g., if X occurs, then I will do Y)" (p. 79). They found that "students who had the opportunity to create implementation intentions demonstrated high performance. Forming implementation intentions to figure out when, where, and how to act toward the target goal can *immunize students from interruptions*" (p. 79; emphasis added). For example, if a student is tempted to check social media while working on their research paper, they can create an implementation intention such as, "If I feel the urge to check social media while writing, then I will first write down my current thought and set a timer for twenty minutes to stay focused on my paper before allowing myself to check my notifications." This plan helps the student stay on track by managing their urge to multitask and dedicating uninterrupted time to their writing.

Finally, *restrictive-choice environments* can help students avoid temptations to switch tasks or attempt to multitask. Restrictive-choice environments may involve actual environments—such as a library, where students know that they will be surrounded by others with the same goals and that distractions will be limited due to a library's norms and rules (Usher & Schunk, 2018)—but they can also be created in other ways. For example, students can:

- Set self-imposed deadlines with costly consequences if they haven't attained a goal by the deadline (Schwartz et al., 2014)
- Engage in more effortful or costly activities to intensify their commitment to a goal (Schumpe, Bélanger, Dugas, Erb, & Kruglanski, 2018)

As an example of setting self-imposed deadlines and consequences, say a student who struggles with completing assignments on time sets a deadline for finishing a research paper by a specific date and commits to donating ten dollars to a charity if they haven't completed the paper by then. This self-imposed financial consequence motivates the student to stay focused and avoid procrastination to ensure they complete the paper on time.

As an example of engaging in more effortful activities to intensify goal commitment, say a student joins a study group where members agree to meet regularly and hold each other accountable. By participating in the group, the student increases their commitment to their study goals, as the regular meetings and shared responsibility make it more challenging to skip study sessions, and they provide additional motivation to stay focused and achieve goals.

Instructional Sequence for Metacognitive Skills

Once students have experienced explicit instruction and modeling for metacognitive strategies, you can continue with guided practice to give them the opportunity to develop expertise with metacognitive skills. As Winne (2018) wrote:

> Learners need help with at least three main tasks: (a) gathering reliable data about how they enacted learning and associating those data with effects, (b) access to tactics and strategies for learning that can be available to metacognitive control and (c) opportunity to practice newer tactics and strategies to bring them to the status of automated skills. (p. 40)

I described six metacognitive strategies in this chapter (three for monitoring and three for control).

1. Evaluate cues (monitoring)
2. Use tools (monitoring)
3. Critique learning (monitoring)
4. Recognize desirable difficulties (control)
5. Practice inhibition (control)
6. Focus on one task (control)

When students are practicing these strategies, provide guidance appropriate to their current level of expertise with each strategy. For example, for students new to *evaluating cues*, start by guiding them through a simple reflection on their recent work, asking them to identify what they felt confident about and what they were unsure of, and helping them see how those feelings might align with their actual performance. For more advanced students, encourage them to compare their self-assessments with peer or teacher feedback, prompting them to refine their understanding of reliable versus unreliable cues.

For students beginning to *use tools* for metacognitive monitoring, provide them with structured prompts like "What do I understand well?" and "What areas do I need more practice in?" and model how to use those prompts effectively. As students become more comfortable, allow them to create their own questions and reflect on their learning progress more independently.

When introducing *recognizing desirable difficulties*, start with simple activities like explaining why a challenging problem or extra practice might be beneficial, using concrete examples to illustrate the concept. As students gain experience, engage them in discussions about different strategies and their long-term benefits, helping them recognize when difficulties are actually opportunities for growth.

For students learning to *practice inhibition*, have them begin by practicing basic tasks like stopping or starting behaviors in structured games or activities. As they improve, incorporate more complex scenarios where they must delay their responses or resist distractions, such as using timers during task completion or practicing patience during decision making.

When students are *focusing on one task*, help beginners by establishing clear boundaries for task focus, such as by designating specific times for study and breaks. For more experienced students, encourage them to create implementation intentions for managing distractions, and challenge them to use restrictive environments, such as by studying in dedicated, distraction-free spaces.

Here's what this looks like in practice: Several days into their unit on photosynthesis, Ms. Williams notices that students are being distracted by unrelated media as they work on their laptops and other devices. At the beginning of the next class period, she says, "You have been making excellent progress in your learning; I'm proud of you. I want to teach you a metacognitive strategy that can make your learning even more efficient and effective: inhibitory control." Ms. Williams then presents the learning progression for inhibitory control shown in figure 4.2 (page 108).

Ms. Williams specifically highlights the process for inhibitory control.

1. Recognize that a situation requires inhibition.
2. Pause and remember your current goal.
3. Calm your body by taking a deep breath or closing your eyes for a moment.
4. Write down or say out loud what you are going to do next.
5. Do what you decided to do.

She also explains when and why to use inhibitory control, along with the other information in the Learning Plan column of figure 4.2. This is explicit instruction.

Then, Ms. Williams asks her students to be on the lookout for situations that require inhibition over the next few class periods. One student shares that they think they can use inhibition today because they are getting distracted by notifications on their computer. Ms. Williams affirms the student's recognition and asks if she could use their situation to demonstrate the process to the class. With the student's consent, Ms. Williams thinks aloud and uses the inhibitory control process to demonstrate how to respond to a media distraction. This is modeling.

Over the next few days and weeks, Ms. Williams periodically asks students if they have noticed a situation requiring inhibitory control. When they have, she asks them to practice the inhibitory control process and provides appropriate feedback, depending on how well each student executes it. This is practice and guidance. Over the following weeks and months, Ms. Williams continues to observe her students and collect data on how often she notices students who are distracted. She is pleased to find that the number of students who succumb to distractions is steadily decreasing.

Procedural Knowledge: *Inhibitory Control*		
	Criteria	**Learning Plan**
Acquisition	List the steps or describe the process. Explain when to use the process. Explain why to use the process.	What are the steps involved in performing this process? 1. Recognize that a situation requires inhibition. 2. Pause and remember your current goal. 3. Calm your body by taking a deep breath or closing your eyes for a moment. 4. Write down or say out loud what you are going to do next. 5. Do what you decided to do. Is the order of the steps important? Yes and no. Some steps, like breathing, pausing, and remembering the goal can happen throughout. Others need to occur in order. When is it appropriate to use this process? When making important decisions During conflicts or disagreements When distractions occur When feeling strong negative emotions, like anger or fear Why is it advantageous to use this process? Inhibitory control can prevent choices with unhealthy or dangerous consequences. It can also promote appropriate and constructive social interactions.
Shaping	Perform the process without errors.	What are common errors made when performing this process? Forgetting to pause (and therefore acting impulsively) Not recognizing that inhibitory control is needed Allowing one's emotions to override one's thinking Being too inhibited or paralyzed (unable to make a decision or select an action) How can errors be avoided when performing this process? Practice mindfulness on a regular basis so calm breathing becomes a habit. Review goals frequently so it is easier to remember them. Manage stress in one's life through appropriate boundaries and personal wellness.
Internalizing	Perform the process at the appropriate rate.	Do I need to learn this process to automaticity, or is controlled processing enough? Automaticity
Utilization	Complete a complex task using this knowledge.	How would this knowledge be used in the real world or in a grown-up job? I am managing my finances. I want to adhere to my budget and invest my savings wisely to create financial stability for myself and my family.

FIGURE 4.2: Sample learning progression for procedural knowledge—Inhibitory control.

*Visit **MarzanoResources.com/reproducibles** for a free reproducible version of this figure.*

Summary

In this chapter, I examined metacognition, which Winne (2022) described as "the engine powering self-regulated learning" (p. 775). I began with the critical role of goals in metacognition and, therefore, in all of self-regulated learning. The good news is that the learning progressions I described in chapter 2 (page 25) are designed to align with the research and theory about how to set appropriate growth goals. After reviewing a process that students can use to set growth goals, I dove into the core metacognitive functions of monitoring and control.

Accurate monitoring is a key ingredient for self-regulated learning because control decisions are based on the judgments students make as a result of data they gather during monitoring. Unfortunately, the cues students use to gather those data are often unreliable. Therefore, I discussed a strategy to help students evaluate cues and prefer those that result in more reliable judgments. I also discussed strategies for effective self-questioning and prompting and how students can engage in self-assessment, all of which are excellent activities for students to collect valid and reliable information about their performance.

Finally, I closed the chapter by examining control strategies. When students make decisions about their next steps and future actions based on monitoring data, they need to recognize that difficult or effortful cognitive strategies are not necessarily ineffective strategies; in fact, they are often the *most effective* strategies. Students need to inhibit the selection of less effective strategies in favor of more effective strategies, even if those strategies require more mental effort to enact. Inhibition also comes into play as students resist the temptation to multitask and focus on the task at hand. I explored specific practice activities that help keep students focused on their goals and immunize them to interruptions and distractions. In the next chapter, I examine the final aspect of self-regulated learning: motivation.

CHAPTER 5
MOTIVATION

Motivation is what gets you moving toward a goal. If metacognition is the engine powering self-regulated learning toward a goal (Winne, 2022), motivation is the fuel. Many researchers and theorists use this (or a similar) analogy to explain motivation, as shown in table 5.1.

TABLE 5.1: Motivation Fuels Self-Regulated Learning

Source	Description of Motivation
Greene, 2018	"Motivation: an omnibus term for the various factors (i.e., cognitive, behavioral, emotional) that fuel the pursuit of goals" (p. 138).
Elliot & Sommet, 2023	"Motivation means the energization and direction of behavior. . . . Energization is the initial impetus or instigator of behavior. . . . Energization represents the 'why' of behavior, the reason that a person is engaged in an action" (pp. 3–4).
Halloun, 2023	"Motivation is the driving force behind pursuing and achieving a specific goal" (p. 109).
Skinner, 2023	"Academic motivation focuses on the 'fire' that fuels students' actions in the educational process" (p. 7).
Urhahne & Wijnia, 2023	"[Motivation] is derived from the Latin word 'movere,' which means 'to move,' as motivation provides the necessary energy to people's actions" (p. 1).

Motivation is necessary for all the other aspects of self-regulated learning to work. To use colloquial language, motivation provides the *will* that causes students to use their *skills*. Greene (2018), commenting on motivational research relative to self-regulated learning, observed that "metacognitive and strategy knowledge was not enough; students had to want to use and transfer this knowledge" (p. 6). Fortunately, there are strategies that students can use to regulate their motivation.

In this chapter, I review four strategies supported by motivation and self-regulation research and theory: (1) act with agency, (2) pursue competence, (3) bolster self-efficacy, and (4) reframe epistemic beliefs. I wrap up the chapter by sharing an instructional sequence for motivational skills.

Strategy 1: Act With Agency

The first strategy that students can leverage to increase their motivation involves cultivating a supportive learning environment by focusing on their personal sense of agency. An *agent* is "someone who acts to improve his or her life circumstances and surroundings" (Reeve et al., 2022, p. 1). Research has found that when students increase their agency, they have a strong potential to change how the teacher interacts with them (Matos, Reeve, Herrera, & Claux, 2018; Patall et al., 2018, 2019; Reeve, 2013). Students can engage in the following actions to increase their sense of agency.

- **Express interests and preferences:** For example, a student might actively share their enthusiasm for environmental science by suggesting a project on climate change solutions.
- **Satisfy curiosity:** For example, if a student is curious about robotics, they could initiate a research project or seek out additional resources on robotics, like clubs or online courses.
- **Develop interests:** For example, a student who is passionate about art might start a personal sketchbook and share their work with peers for feedback. They can also seek out art classes or local art shows to further develop their skills and knowledge in their area of interest.
- **Build a sense of competence:** For example, if a student feels they are improving in a particular skill, such as coding, they could challenge themselves by taking on a more complex project or creating a personal app.

- **Attain personal goals:** For example, a student who wants to improve their writing skills might set a goal to write and revise a short story. They could track their progress by seeking feedback from teachers or peers.
- **Take personal initiative:** For example, if a student identifies a need for better study resources in their classroom, they might take the initiative to create and distribute study guides for their classmates.

These actions on the students' part result in a more supportive learning environment because they make teachers more aware of students' wants, needs, and interests. In turn, teachers are then in a better position to present content in ways that are relevant to the preferences that students have expressed (Matos et al., 2018).

You should not expect students to naturally take these actions; most students will need you to prompt them. This sort of teaching approach, where the teacher instructs students about how to increase their agency in the classroom, has a name—autonomy-supportive teaching—and a research base. Johnmarshall Reeve and Sung Hyeon Cheon (2021) conducted a review of research on autonomy-supportive teachers and found that their students enjoyed increases in the following areas.

- Need satisfaction
- Intrinsic motivation
- Internalization of school values
- Classroom engagement
- Perceived skills development
- Self-regulated learning
- Positive emotions
- Well-being
- Positive self-concept
- Academic achievement and course grades

Students of autonomy-supportive teachers also experienced less need frustration, amotivation, controlled motivation, disengagement, negative feelings, and problematic peer relationships. Researchers Julien S. Bureau, Joshua L. Howard, Jane X. Y. Chong, and Frédéric Guay (2022) meta-analyzed 144 studies involving over seventy-nine thousand students and found that autonomy support from teachers correlates more strongly with student motivation than autonomy support from parents (0.48 for teachers versus 0.23 for parents).

As simple as it seems, the very best way to help students increase their agency is to explicitly tell them to take the actions I listed previously. Reeve and colleagues (2022) evaluated an intervention where students were simply given the following three directions (which were based on previous studies and observations of highly agentic students).

1. Show initiative; don't wait for the teacher to tell you what to do.
2. Speak up and let the teacher know what you are interested in.
3. Ask questions to help you learn.

They found that giving students these directions had a "direct, causal effect on creating a more supportive learning environment for oneself" (Reeve et al., 2022, p. 8). Therefore, to help students create a more supportive learning environment for themselves, first provide explicit instruction about the actions that can help them do that (as I listed previously), and model what each one looks like (or ask students to model it). Then, as students are engaged in learning tasks, give them appropriate guidance so they practice using each action. For example, you might start a classroom discussion by explicitly instructing students to express their interests and preferences. After explaining the importance of showing initiative, you could prompt them to share their ideas for a project on a topic they are passionate about. You could then model how to articulate interests effectively and encourage students to take the lead in proposing project ideas or asking questions about topics they want to explore further. As students work on their learning goals, you might prompt them to ask questions or give them a tracking scheme so they can track their own use of questions while learning.

Strategy 2: Pursue Competence

In the previously cited meta-analysis by Bureau and colleagues (2022), there was an additional finding that is critical for students to understand during self-regulated learning. The strongest predictor of the most powerful types of student motivation (Howard, Bureau, Guay, Chong, & Ryan, 2021) was the need for competence. *Competence* is a person's need to grow, succeed, and feel effective, and it is one of the three basic psychological needs that psychologists Edward L. Deci and Richard M. Ryan postulated (1987, 2000, 2012; Ryan & Deci, 2000a, 2000b, 2009, 2017, 2020) in their *self-determination theory*. As the theory goes, human beings need three things to be motivated and experience well-being: (1) autonomy, (2) competence, and (3) relatedness. And the greatest of these is competence (according to Bureau et al., 2022; for similar findings, see also Levesque-Bristol, Richards, Zissimopoulos, Wang, & Yu, 2022; Vasconcellos et al., 2020).

Lisette Hornstra, Kim Stroet, Christine Rubie-Davies, and Annaline Flint (2023) identified specific classroom structures and processes that support students' need for competence, including the following.

- Clear and consistent guidelines about desired outcomes
- Guidance about how to achieve desired outcomes (step-by-step directions)
- Feedback and materials that vary according to the level of the learner
- Feedback and materials that vary according to the choices a learner makes
- Optimal challenges based on a student's current level of performance
- Availability of help, proactive encouragement, and specific feedback

Utilizing the processes I offered in the early chapters of this book will likely result in these conditions, as evidenced by the research cited thus far. Specifically, the learning progressions that students articulate (as I described in chapter 2, page 25) provide clear and consistent guidelines about desired outcomes and help students identify optimal challenges based on their current level of performance. The cognitive strategies I presented in chapter 3 (page 47) provide guidance about how to achieve the outcomes at each performance level on a learning progression. The instructional sequence in chapter 1 (page 7) and the learning progression in chapter 2 are designed to help you provide feedback and materials that vary according to the learner's level. By implementing the processes in this book, you will already be well on your way to supporting your students as they pursue competence. However, there's more they can do.

Competence-driven motivation is largely based on students' beliefs (Usher, 2016) about (1) whether they will be successful at a task and (2) whether a task is worth their time and energy (Eccles & Wigfield, 2020). These beliefs can be conceptualized as students' answers to the two following questions.

1. Can I do this task?
2. Is this task worth doing?

If students answer no to either question, motivation is threatened (Fréchette-Simard, Plante, Duchesne, & Chaffee, 2022). What is the point of engaging in a task if (1) you don't think you can succeed at it or (2) you don't think it's worth succeeding at?

During self-regulated learning, students need to recognize if they don't think they can do a task or if they think a task isn't worth doing. Because either of those beliefs threatens motivation, students also need to know how to change their beliefs. Although you might think that changing a belief is nearly impossible, research—summarized by Kuhn (2022)—has found that asking people to explain what underlies their beliefs can reduce their certainty about those beliefs, leaving the door open for conceptual change. Additionally, students with higher inhibitory control (addressed in chapter 4, page 75) are better able to relinquish unproductive or faulty beliefs (Butterfuss & Kendeou, 2020). The next two strategies I present—bolster self-efficacy and reframe epistemic beliefs—are designed to help students think more deeply about why they answered no (if they did) to one of the two previous questions and whether they should change that no to a yes.

Strategy 3: Bolster Self-Efficacy

If students don't think they can do a task, they should examine and seek to bolster their self-efficacy beliefs. Bandura coined the term *self-efficacy* in 1977. According to Hyun Ji Lee and Mimi Bong (2023), self-efficacy "represents one's personal conviction about her or his capability to successfully perform a specific task at the desired level" (p. 250). Most importantly, "it is a subjective judgment and, as such, does not necessarily reflect one's actual capabilities" (p. 250). As with metacognitive monitoring skills, self-efficacy beliefs are not an innately human characteristic or something that suddenly emerges. Rather, students gather information from sources to form their self-efficacy beliefs. Specifically, self-efficacy beliefs are based on information drawn from four sources (Schunk & Usher, 2019; Usher, Ford, Li, & Weidner, 2019).

1. *Performance accomplishments*, such as successfully completing a challenging science project (positive) or experiencing a failed lab experiment (negative).
2. *Observations of similar others*, such as seeing a classmate figure out how to solve quadratic equations (positive) or watching a classmate struggle to learn mathematics facts (negative).
3. *Persuasive verbal statements*, such as receiving positive feedback from a teacher about writing skills (positive) or receiving negative feedback from a peer about a presentation (negative).
4. *Physiological or emotional feelings*, such as feeling calm and focused after preparing for a speech (positive) or feeling anxious and scared before an assessment (negative).

Each of these sources of information can be engineered, thus providing an opportunity for students to influence (and change) their self-efficacy beliefs. The most important source of information is performance accomplishments.

The term *performance accomplishments* is another way of saying you accomplished a goal. When you accomplish a goal, your self-efficacy increases. Thus, setting appropriate goals (as I described in chapter 4, page 75) and tracking progress toward them (as I described in chapter 2, page 25) are critical steps toward positive self-efficacy beliefs. As Dale H. Schunk and Maria K. DiBenedetto (2020) explained, "Heightened self-efficacy should result from the observation of learning progress" (p. 5). Given the importance of performance accomplishments, I want to address here how students respond to errors, because errors have the potential to throw students off track from accomplishing their goals. Thomas Goetz and colleagues (2023) explained, "It is important to make clear to students that errors and mistakes should be regarded as opportunities to learn, and that abilities are malleable" (p. 156). Helping students develop a healthy relationship with errors strengthens their self-efficacy defenses. One strategy for this is to teach students to use deliberate erring.

Deliberate erring involves "deliberately committing and correcting errors" (Wong, 2023, p. 2) and has been shown to benefit learning in many ways (Hays, Kornell, & Bjork, 2013; Kapur, 2014, 2016; Kornell, Hays, & Bjork, 2009; Mera, Rodríguez, & Marin-Garcia, 2022; Metcalfe, 2017; Metcalfe & Xu, 2018; Potts, Davies, & Shanks, 2019; Potts & Shanks, 2014; Wong & Lim, 2022a, 2022b). Sarah Shi Hui Wong and Stephen Wee Hun Lim (2022a) reported that "deliberate erring enhances learning, even when one already knows the correct answers" (p. 1818). Such an approach can minimize the detrimental potential of errors by "allowing learners to veridically attribute their errors to the learning approach rather than dispositional factors" (p. 1818). To use deliberate erring, one of the simplest approaches is to have students complete this sentence stem about the knowledge they are currently working with: "People might think that ________, but actually, ________." For example, a student studying photosynthesis might complete the sentence stem as follows: "People might think that plants only need sunlight to perform photosynthesis, but actually, they also require carbon dioxide from the air and water from the soil."

While less significant than performance accomplishments, *observations of similar others* are also important contributions to self-efficacy. A simple but effective way to facilitate observations of similar others is through celebrations; drawing attention to the positive accomplishments of peers can increase a student's self-efficacy. When you see someone like you (in age, ethnicity, race, gender, and so on) accomplish a goal, your belief that you can accomplish the same goal (your self-efficacy) increases. As Schunk and DiBenedetto (2023) explained, "Observing similar others succeed can raise observers' self-efficacy and motivate them to try the task; they are apt to believe that if others can do it, they can as well" (p. 27). Lee and Bong (2023) stated that "performances of peers who share similar backgrounds and characteristics with oneself can be more informative than those of peers who do not" (p. 251). When celebrating students' accomplishments, it is important to have the student share what they did to achieve their goal. Not only does this give students who are observing ideas of actions they might take on their way to the same goal, but it reinforces the overall belief that there is a correlation between the effort expended and the outcomes achieved. For example, if a student composes an exceptionally effective persuasive essay, highlight their achievement by having them share their piece with the class. The student being celebrated should also share the strategies they used to produce the essay, such as their approach to organizing ideas, revising drafts, and seeking feedback.

Persuasive verbal statements come with an important caveat: They must be credible (Schunk & DiBenedetto, 2016). That is, as Lee and Bong (2023) explained, "Persuasions could provide an effective means to strengthen one's self-efficacy when combined with multifaceted strategies to develop actual skills" (p. 251). This means that generic statements such as "You can do it!" are not as effective as specific statements that praise specific strategies and skills. For example, say instead, "I noticed that you improved your problem-solving skills by breaking down the complex equations into smaller, manageable steps. Keep using this approach; it's helping you tackle even the most challenging problems effectively. Your ability to analyze and solve these problems will only get stronger with practice."

Finally, *physiological or emotional feelings* play a role in self-efficacy and, in truth, all of motivation (Pekrun, 2023). Positive emotions signal to students that things are going well; negative emotions signal to students that they are not (Carver & Scheier, 2019). Students can regulate their emotions toward positivity to facilitate achievement of their goals (English, Lee, John, & Gross, 2017; Thompson, 2019). One strategy for this involves making physiological, mental, and relational choices that promote positive emotions (Ng et al., 2022). For example, a student might feel disappointed with their performance on an assessment. Instead of ruminating about the mistakes they made, they choose to breathe deeply, inhibit their negative thoughts, and seek support and positive affirmations from their friends. These choices regulate the student's emotions and allow them to more effectively focus on the learning they need to do for the rest of the day. Another strategy is called *attributional retraining* (Linnenbrink-Garcia, Patall, & Pekrun, 2016). Researchers Lara Forsblom, Reinhard Pekrun, Kristina Loderer, and Francisco Peixoto (2022) explained that this approach "guides students to attribute their failures to internal, unstable, and controllable causes (e.g., lack of effort, poor strategy use) rather than internal, stable, and uncontrollable causes (e.g., low ability; Linnenbrink-Garcia et al., 2016; Perry et al., 2014)" (p. 363). For example, if a student receives negative feedback about a project, instead of viewing it as a reflection of their overall ability, they attribute the result to not spending enough time on research and not using the most effective study strategies. This perspective helps the student focus on specific areas for improvement, such as exercising better time management or seeking additional resources rather than feeling helpless or believing they lack the inherent ability to succeed.

Each of the strategies associated with a source of self-efficacy beliefs can help students focus on pursuing competence in situations where their self-efficacy is low. These strategies help students revisit their beliefs about whether they can successfully complete a task and bolster their self-efficacy as needed. However, sometimes the threat to competence involves students' beliefs about the value of a task. When students answer no to the question "Is this task worth doing?" they will likely need to reframe their epistemic beliefs, which I address next.

Strategy 4: Reframe Epistemic Beliefs

Epistemic beliefs refers to how a person thinks about knowledge. According to McCarthy and McNamara (2023), epistemic beliefs involve "the degree to which a person views knowledge as certain or uncertain, simple or complex, whether knowledge or truth is derived internally by the individual or externally through authority" (p. 211). Epistemic beliefs develop through three fairly well-defined phases over the course of a person's life (Iordanou, 2022), as described in table 5.2 (page 120).

Epistemic beliefs contribute to the relative value students place on different tasks. For example, an absolutist or a multiplist will not likely place a high value on constructing arguments (an analysis task). In contrast, "evaluativists view argumentation as a valuable activity to engage in to help them form a judgment on an issue" (Iordanou, 2022, p. 403).

Notice that the third column of table 5.2 denotes the age during which students typically hold absolutist, multiplist, and evaluativist beliefs. You might argue that young children don't need to be taught to reframe their epistemic beliefs because they are not developmentally ready to do so. However, I would submit an argument that neuroscientist Adele Diamond (2016) made regarding students' executive functions, which—like epistemic beliefs—do not fully develop until late adolescence:

TABLE 5.2: Development of Epistemic Beliefs

Level	Descriptors	Typical Developmental Age
Absolutism	Truth is objective. Individuals are either right or wrong. Alternative claims are discussed as false beliefs requiring correction.	Childhood
Multiplism	Knowledge is subjective. Evidence can be interpreted differently and can support different beliefs and theories. Multiple opinions may exist on an issue; we can choose to agree to disagree instead of discussing these opinions.	Adolescence
Evaluativism	Knowledge is judgment. We must evaluate alternative positions to find the best model supported by the available evidence and data. Knowledge is subject to change if new evidence or a more powerfully explanatory model or theory becomes available.	Adolescence to adulthood

Source: Iordanou, 2022.

> I think it is helpful to consider an analogy. Certainly toddlers' legs are not at their full adult extent, and they probably will not be for another 15 years or so, but with those immature legs toddlers can walk and even run. That is to say that even though the prefrontal cortex is immature, it is able to subserve [executive functions] to some extent (not at the full adult level, but to some extent) and with training and practice, that immature prefrontal cortex can probably subserve [executive functions] at a higher level of proficiency. (pp. 20–21)

Young children may not be able to fully realize multiplist or evaluativist epistemic beliefs, but if you introduce them to the fact that such possibilities exist and ask them to practice with them, they are likely to use epistemic beliefs with a higher level of proficiency in the present and in the future.

Students can examine their current epistemic beliefs by articulating why they think each performance level (for both declarative and procedural knowledge) is important. If they are unable to do so, or if they think that a particular performance level is unnecessary or unimportant, they should aim to learn more about why that performance level is important to reframe their epistemic beliefs about it.

For example, if a student believes that analysis tasks for declarative knowledge (such as examining relationships) are unnecessary because they feel they only need to know the facts, they could explore how analysis tasks help deepen their understanding and lead to more complex, integrated knowledge. Similarly, if a student thinks shaping tasks for procedural knowledge are unimportant, they might learn about how practicing a process with high accuracy ensures that they learn it correctly, which prevents the reinforcement of errors and supports successful internalizing and utilizing of the process later.

Instructional Sequence for Motivational Skills

In this chapter, I examined four strategies that students can use to keep their motivation high during self-regulated learning.

1. Act with agency.
2. Pursue competence.
3. Bolster self-efficacy.
4. Reframe epistemic beliefs.

As with the strategies I presented in previous chapters, these strategies are procedural knowledge, which can be taught using the instructional sequence I presented in chapter 1 (page 7). For example, to teach students to *act with agency*, start with explicit instruction by explaining that acting with agency (what) should be used whenever possible (when) because doing so helps them feel more in control and motivated (why). Give them a list of actions that they can use to act with agency (how), then note that acting with agency is procedural knowledge, for which the steps do not need to be performed in order. Model this by choosing a project topic yourself, thinking aloud about the decision-making process and demonstrating how making a choice impacts your engagement. Have students practice by selecting their own topics or learning strategies for the knowledge they are working on, then reflecting on their choices and outcomes. Provide guidance by offering a decision-making checklist (general guidance) or prompts (specific guidance) that encourage them to consider how their choices affect their motivation and learning.

To teach students to *pursue competence*, begin by explicitly instructing them on how to pursue competence (what), which involves setting growth goals (how). Students should pursue competence as much as possible (when) because it improves their overall well-being and satisfaction with life (why). Model this by setting a growth goal for yourself, breaking it down into smaller steps, and showing how to track progress. Let students practice setting and tracking their own growth goals using goal-setting worksheets (general guidance). Offer additional guidance by providing feedback on their goals and progress, using prompts (specific guidance) to help them reflect on their achievements and adjust their goals as needed.

Explicitly teach students how to *bolster self-efficacy* (what) whenever they answer no to the question "Can I do this task?" (when). Explain that high self-efficacy helps them persist through challenges and stay motivated (why) and teach them the strategy of deliberate erring to help inoculate them against the negative effects of errors on performance accomplishments (how). Model this by demonstrating how to fill in the deliberate erring sentence stem for different types of content. Have students practice deliberate erring for the content they are currently working on and ask them to think about what performance levels they think this strategy is best suited to. Provide guidance by using prompts to help them identify their strengths and past successes, offering feedback on their use of self-efficacy strategies, and suggesting improvements as needed.

For *reframing epistemic beliefs*, start with explicit instruction on the different types of epistemic beliefs (what) and explain that how you think about knowledge can affect how valuable you think a learning task is (why). Tell students that if they answer no to the question "Is this task worth doing?" (when), they should do some research to find out why their current performance level is important to their learning of the knowledge they're working on. Model this by sharing a personal experience where changing your beliefs about learning helped you overcome difficulties. Have students reflect on their own beliefs about learning and practice reframing challenges as opportunities for growth. Provide guidance by offering examples of common misconceptions about learning (general guidance) and how to reframe them, using prompts (specific guidance) to encourage students to apply these reframing strategies to their own experiences.

Here's what this looks like in practice: As Ms. Williams's class nears the end of the unit on photosynthesis, she notices that many of her students seem reluctant to move to the utilization level of performance. She shares this observation with them and asks them if they perceive the same thing, and why they think that might be happening. Several students affirm that they are intimidated by the complexities of figuring out how to use their knowledge of photosynthesis to address larger problems in agricultural science; they're not sure they can do that very well. Ms. Williams thanks these students for sharing and decides to teach the class procedural knowledge related to bolstering self-efficacy. First, she presents the learning progression for bolstering self-efficacy shown in figure 5.1.

<table>
<tr><th colspan="3">Procedural Knowledge: Bolstering Self-Efficacy</th></tr>
<tr><th></th><th>Criteria</th><th>Learning Plan</th></tr>
<tr><td>Acquisition</td><td>List the steps or describe the process.

Explain when to use the process.

Explain why to use the process.</td><td>What are the steps involved in performing this process?
1. Recognize when you think you can't do something.
2. Decide if you want to do the thing you think you can't do. If you want to do it, set a goal to do it.
3. Find other people who have already accomplished the goal and ask them how they did it.
4. Create a series of small tasks you think you can do that will get you to your goal.
5. Do each small task. After you succeed at it, celebrate your success with positive self-talk and with others.
6. Make adjustments when you need to. If you make a mistake, correct it.
7. When you achieve your goal, celebrate!
Is the order of the steps important?
Generally, yes. But you will likely need to cycle through steps 5 and 6 several times before you achieve your goal.
When is it appropriate to use this process?
When facing difficult tasks or after a setback or failure
When learning new information or skills
Before high-stakes situations (like exams or presentations)
During times of transition or change
Why is it advantageous to use this process?
High self-efficacy increases motivation, persistence, and performance.
High self-efficacy reduces stress and anxiety.</td></tr>
<tr><td>Shaping</td><td>Perform the process without errors.</td><td>What are common errors made when performing this process?
Focusing too much on past failures or the failures of others
Pursuing goals that you don't really want or need to achieve
Ignoring small victories or forgetting to use positive self-talk
Comparing yourself to others rather than using your internal standards for success
How can errors be avoided when performing this process?
Seek positive and constructive feedback from trusted people.
Adopt an attitude of curiosity and aim for personal growth rather than comparisons to others.
Prioritize your well-being by getting enough sleep, exercising, and eating healthy food.</td></tr>
</table>

FIGURE 5.1: Sample learning progression for procedural knowledge—Bolstering self-efficacy.

continued →

	Criteria	Learning Plan
Internalizing	Perform the process at the appropriate rate.	Do I need to learn this process to automaticity, or is controlled processing enough? Automaticity
Utilization	Complete a complex task using this knowledge.	How would this knowledge be used in the real world or in a grown-up job? I am the manager of a team at work. I need to make a plan so that we can meet a big goal that seems daunting.

Visit ***MarzanoResources.com/reproducibles*** *for a free reproducible version of this figure.*

Ms. Williams draws students' attention to the process for bolstering self-efficacy.

1. Recognize when you think you can't do something.
2. Decide if you want to do the thing you think you can't do. If you want to do it, set a goal to do it.
3. Find other people who have already accomplished the goal and ask them how they did it.
4. Create a series of small tasks you think you can do that will get you to your goal.
5. Do each small task. After you succeed at it, celebrate your success with positive self-talk and with others.
6. Make adjustments when you need to. If you make a mistake, correct it.
7. When you achieve your goal, celebrate!

She also explains when and why students should bolster their self-efficacy and reviews the other information in the Learning Plan column of figure 5.1 (page 123). This is explicit instruction.

Then, Ms. Williams asks each student to remember a time when they thought they couldn't achieve a goal. One student raises their hand to share a memory. This student plays ice hockey and recently missed a potentially game-winning goal right when the buzzer sounded. They have started to doubt their ability to perform under pressure during upcoming games. Ms. Williams receives the student's permission to use their situation to model bolstering self-efficacy and thinks aloud as she demonstrates the process. This is modeling.

Finally, Ms. Williams asks each student to use the process for bolstering self-efficacy to write or record a journal entry recounting a time when they thought they couldn't accomplish a goal. Ms. Williams briefly reviews these entries after class and plans to provide guidance to students based on their level of expertise with the process. This is practice and guidance. The following class period, Ms. Williams asks students in the class who have not yet addressed the utilization level of performance for photosynthesis to use the bolstering self-efficacy process to make a plan for that goal.

Summary

In this chapter, I examined a huge psychological construct—motivation—that is critical to self-regulated learning. If students aren't motivated to engage in learning, it doesn't matter how many strategies they have in knowledge, cognition, or metacognition—self-regulated learning just won't happen. Therefore, I presented four strategies that you can teach students to use to manage their motivation during self-regulated learning. Acting with agency involves taking charge of your experience and engaging in actions and choices that will foster a supportive learning environment for yourself. Students who act agentically create the conditions for autonomy-supportive teaching, an approach that has been shown to improve students' motivation and feelings of competence. I recommended that you explicitly teach students how to pursue competence by having them ask themselves two questions as they approach a task: (1) "Can I do this task?" and (2) "Is this task worth doing?" If students answer no to either question, they should pause and take steps to bolster their self-efficacy (if they answered no to the first question) or to reframe their epistemic beliefs (if they answered no to the second question). While some may think that beliefs cannot be changed, research indicates otherwise. There are specific steps and strategies that students can use to realize more productive beliefs, both about themselves and about the learning tasks they engage in.

EPILOGUE

As I explored self-regulated learning, one of my favorite analogies was Winne's (2018, 2022) description of students engaged in self-regulated learning as "learning scientists." He whimsically described students as "the principal investigators in a personal program of research" (Winne, 2018, p. 40) and somewhat pessimistically referred to the disadvantages they face in that endeavor:

> Their research is disadvantaged by erratic records about how they learn, and a tiny and biased sample of *N* = me. . . . They are ill-prepared and under-resourced. . . . Incentives are slight to cast aside "good enough" learning strategies and spend dear effort deliberately practicing risky but potentially more effective tactics and strategies on a path to forging automated routines. (Winne, 2022, pp. 774, 785)

I love this picture of students as young scientists, studying their own learning. When I taught, I loved watching my students' energy rise when they figured out a strategy that worked for them. But I saw the challenges, as well, both for myself and my students. There is so much knowledge articulated in standards that it is difficult to carve out time to teach students to be learners and learning scientists. When a student is behind, it is counterintuitive to take time away from literacy or mathematics to teach self-regulated learning. As a teacher, self-regulated learning sounded awesome to me, but it also seemed like a big, complicated thing. Students and teachers often don't know where to start. But I think there is hope. Students *can* succeed at the endeavor of being learning scientists, and you can empower them to do it. It starts with understanding the nature of knowledge and how different kinds of knowledge are learned. After reviewing the research and theory in chapter 1 (page 7), this is where we started in chapter 2 (page 25).

The research on rubrics provides excellent guidance about how to set students up for success in self-regulated learning. Learning progressions articulate knowledge items as a set of criteria at escalating performance levels. For declarative knowledge, students acquire, organize, analyze, and utilize knowledge. For procedural knowledge, students acquire, shape, internalize, and utilize knowledge. Students can write their own learning progressions—thus previewing the content—and use them to track their progress toward growth goals.

In chapter 3 (page 47), I expanded on the performance levels I presented in the previous chapter, providing specific cognitive strategies that students can use to learn knowledge at each level. The strategies in chapter 3 all have long tails of research demonstrating their efficacy in a wide variety of contexts with a wide range of content. But students could also utilize high-return-on-investment strategies—those that require little investment and have the potential to produce great learning gains. Whenever you or your students use a strategy, leverage the action-research process I articulated in the introduction to examine whether it is producing the desired outcome.

In chapter 4 (page 75), we finally got to the topic that started my self-regulated learning journey: metacognition. Students use metacognitive strategies to monitor their learning ("Is this working?") and control their learning ("What will I do if it's not working?"). Students can use specific strategies to ensure they are accurately judging their learning as they pursue their goals. You can empower them to make productive control decisions, especially about the cognitive strategies they choose to use as they twist and turn through the dance of self-regulated learning.

Finally, in chapter 5 (page 111), we closed with motivation, the fuel that drives the whole process. Motivation isn't up to chance or the vagaries of personal interests and preferences. Students can regulate it using specific strategies that go to the heart of their beliefs about themselves, their learning, and their ability to improve their situation. Throughout all the chapters, I exemplified and described how to use the instructional sequence from chapter 1 (page 7) to teach the specific skills that students need to engage in during self-regulated learning.

In closing, I'll both agree and disagree with Allyson Hadwin (2021). She stated that:

> Self-regulated learning is not an outcome; it is a dynamic process unfolding over time, tasks, and domains. . . . Self-regulating learners are characterized as individuals who can strategically adapt learning, motivation, emotions, and behaviors when new challenges or situations arise that compromise goal attainment. (p. 1)

I agree with everything she said except for that first bit. I think self-regulated learning *can be* an outcome. Or, rather, I think self-regulated learning can be conceptualized as a set of outcomes—a menu of strategies and information that can be explicitly taught to and practiced by students. This book is my effort to articulate that menu of strategies and information. My greatest hope is that it will be useful to you as you cultivate self-regulated learners in your classroom. As always, thank you for all you do.

APPENDIX

The following table contains a list of the cognitive strategies from chapter 3 (page 47) as well as suggestions for incorporating them into regular classroom practice.

COGNITIVE STRATEGY: **Retrieval practice**

PERFORMANCE LEVEL: **Acquisition**

How to Incorporate It Into Classroom Practice:

- **Low-stakes quizzing:** Begin each class or lesson with a short set of questions about previously learned content.
- **Flash cards:** Provide premade sets of flash cards that students can use to quiz themselves or peers on facts, vocabulary terms, and concepts.
- **Peer quizzing:** Pair students up and have them take turns asking each other questions about the content.
- **Technology:** Use online platforms or apps like Quizlet (https://quizlet.com) or Kahoot! (https://kahoot.com) to make practice tests engaging and interactive.
- **Exit tickets:** Have students write down key points or answers to questions at the end of a class or lesson.
- **Brain dumps:** Ask students to write down or tell a partner everything they remember about a topic without using resources.
- **Timed recall:** Give students a set amount of time to write down as many facts, terms, or concepts as they can about a topic.

- **Question banks:** Create a set of questions related to the content and give students access to it.
- **Gamification:** Play trivia- or Jeopardy-style games in a low-stakes and just-for-fun way.

COGNITIVE STRATEGY: **Concept mapping**

PERFORMANCE LEVEL: **Organization**

How to Incorporate It Into Classroom Practice:

- **Software:** Use digital tools to allow students to create and share online concept maps.
- **Visual aids:** Incorporate concept maps into your instructional materials, such as slides or handouts.
- **Examples:** Ask your colleagues to make concept maps about an aspect of the content they teach and post them in a location where students can browse them.
- **Competitions:** Organize friendly competitions where groups create concept maps on a specific topic, which are then judged on creativity, accuracy, and complexity.
- **Flipped classroom:** After students watch a video or read a text as homework, ask them to create a concept map to organize the content. Share these in class.
- **Journals:** Have students keep a journal where they regularly create and update maps related to the topics they are learning.
- **Collective concept maps:** Create a large interactive map in the classroom where students can add elements using sticky notes and string.
- **Scaffolded maps:** Provide partially completed concept maps at the start of a lesson and ask students to fill in the missing pieces.

COGNITIVE STRATEGY: **Generative learning**

PERFORMANCE LEVEL: **Organization**

How to Incorporate It Into Classroom Practice:

- **Elaborative interrogation:** Ask students to explain why they think certain relationships exist among content elements.
- **Peer teaching:** After answering a question and before the correct answer is revealed, ask students to explain to a peer why they think the answer they gave is correct.
- **Paraphrasing:** Ask students to restate material in their own words.
- **Structure argumentation:** Select two different structures for the content students are learning that they could use to organize the content, and have different students or groups defend a structure.
- **Think-pair-share:** After presenting content, ask students to select the structure they'd use to organize it and explain why to a partner before sharing with the class.
- **Role playing:** Have students take on the roles of historical figures, scientists, or characters and explain how those people might organize content, given what was known when they were alive.
- **Presentations:** Have students design a slide deck that they can use to explain why they chose a specific organizational structure for the content they are learning.

COGNITIVE STRATEGY: **Examining relationships**

PERFORMANCE LEVEL: **Analysis**

How to Incorporate It Into Classroom Practice:

- **Causes:** Ask students to name the causes of a historical event, a scientific phenomenon, a mathematical breakthrough, or a literary work.
- **Similarities or differences:** In a friendly competition, ask one team to find as many similarities between two concepts as possible, while the opposing team finds as many differences as possible.

- **Parts of a system:** In a friendly competition, ask teams to alternate naming a single part of a system and explaining how it interacts with other parts. When neither team can think of any more parts, the last team who named a part wins.

COGNITIVE STRATEGY: **Evaluating information**

PERFORMANCE LEVEL: **Analysis**

How to Incorporate It Into Classroom Practice:

- **FACT testing:** Whenever students access information online, ask them to subject it to the FACT test (adapted from Blakeslee, 2004).
    - *Facts*—Are they accurate? Is there evidence? Are specific and clear details given?
    - *Authority*—Who is the author? What are their credentials? Who published this? Is it biased?
    - *Content*—Is it relevant? Is the coverage in depth? Are multiple perspectives represented?
    - *Timeliness*—When was this published or updated? Has anything changed since this was published?
- **Primary and secondary sources:** When students share information, ask them to identify whether the information came from a primary or secondary source.
- **Author ID:** When students share information, ask them to identify the author and give that person's credentials or bio.
- **Technology:** Introduce students to fact-checking websites like Snopes (www.snopes.com), FactCheck.org (www.factcheck.org), or PolitiFact (www.politifact.com).
- **Bias binge:** Ask students to find examples of biased material in the media. Designate a time for them to share what they found in class.

COGNITIVE STRATEGY: **Constructing arguments**

PERFORMANCE LEVEL: **Analysis**

How to Incorporate It Into Classroom Practice:

- **Informal debates:** Whenever content offers more than one perspective, have students informally take positions and briefly debate the topic.
- **Socratic seminars:** Prompt students to ask questions designed to find out what their peers think about a topic.
- **Framework:** Present a framework for arguments that shows how claims, evidence, and reasoning relate to each other (such as the one shown in figure 3.1, page 56).

COGNITIVE STRATEGY: **Interleaved practice**

PERFORMANCE LEVEL: **Shaping**

How to Incorporate It Into Classroom Practice:

- **Interleaved teaching:** Identify concepts that you can interleave for instruction, such as addition and subtraction.
- **Mixed practice:** Provide sets of practice problems for students that include several different types of problems.
- **Technology:** Use interactive tools and apps that allow you and your students to design quizzes and exercises that mix various skills.
- **Integrated content:** If you teach more than one content area to the same students, find ways to integrate topics, such as weather and probability or plants and measurement.
- **Practice problems:** While working on one topic—for example, a science experiment—have students pause and complete a few practice problems for a different but related concept, such as balancing chemical equations.

COGNITIVE STRATEGY: **Spaced practice**

PERFORMANCE LEVEL: **Internalizing**

How to Incorporate It Into Classroom Practice:

- **Review schedules:** Work with students to create a schedule for reviewing previously learned concepts, scheduling several weeks to several months into the future.
- **Designated time:** Set aside time each week for students to practice previously learned skills, with the goal of increasing their speed while maintaining accuracy.
- **Warm-ups:** At the beginning of each class or lesson, ask students to practice a skill related to the content.
- **Technology:** Use apps and online platforms that allow students to set a schedule for practice sessions.
- **Paired practice:** Give students the opportunity to practice with a peer, where one student practices and the other student collects data and gives feedback.
- **At-home practice:** Task students to practice previously learned skills as a regular homework activity.

COGNITIVE STRATEGY: **Decision making**

PERFORMANCE LEVEL: **Utilization**

How to Incorporate It Into Classroom Practice:

- Teach students a process for decision making, such as the following.
    1. **Identify the decision:** Clearly understand the decision you need to make.
    2. **Gather information:** Research the decision, including background information, options, and potential impacts.
    3. **Generate alternatives:** List possible choices, including the pros and cons of each option.
    4. **Make a decision:** Choose the best alternative based on the pros and cons of each.
    5. **Implement and review:** Execute your choice. If things don't go as you expected, you may need to re-evaluate and, if possible, make a different choice.

COGNITIVE STRATEGY: **Problem solving**

PERFORMANCE LEVEL: **Utilization**

How to Incorporate It Into Classroom Practice:

- Teach students a process for problem solving, such as the following.
    1. **Understand the problem:** Clearly define what the problem is and what you need to solve.
    2. **Collect data:** Gather relevant information. You may need to research, observe, or consult with others.
    3. **Brainstorm solutions:** Develop a list of possible solutions. Consider all possible options, even those that might seem impractical.
    4. **Assess options:** Evaluate each possible solution, considering the benefits and drawbacks of each.
    5. **Implement a solution:** Choose a solution and put it in place. If things don't go as you expected, you may need to re-evaluate and, if possible, adjust the solution.

COGNITIVE STRATEGY: **Invention**

PERFORMANCE LEVEL: **Utilization**

How to Incorporate It Into Classroom Practice:

- Teach students a process for invention, such as the following.
    1. **Identify an opportunity:** Look for gaps that highlight a need. What isn't working well?
    2. **Generate ideas:** Develop several concepts that could address the gap or need.
    3. **Refine concepts:** Create preliminary designs or prototypes of your ideas.
    4. **Evaluate prototypes:** Based on effectiveness, feasibility, and cost, decide which prototype is the most promising.
    5. **Finalize and launch:** Develop the final version of your invention and present it to the intended audience.

COGNITIVE STRATEGY: **Experimentation**

PERFORMANCE LEVEL: **Utilization**

How to Incorporate It Into Classroom Practice:

- Teach students a process for experimentation, such as the following.
    1. **Ask a research question:** Identify a question or hypothesis that can be addressed using an experiment.
    2. **Design the experiment:** Develop a plan for how you will test your research question, including defining variables, designing a procedure, and preparing to collect and analyze data.
    3. **Conduct the experiment:** Follow your plan to carry out the test, making observations and collecting data as you do so.
    4. **Analyze data:** Look for patterns, relationships, or significant differences in the data, using statistical methods if appropriate.
    5. **Draw conclusions and communicate findings:** Based on your analysis of the data, draw conclusions and articulate them as claims, using your experiment to provide evidence for those claims.

COGNITIVE STRATEGY: **Investigation**

PERFORMANCE LEVEL: **Utilization**

How to Incorporate It Into Classroom Practice:

- Teach students a process for investigation, such as the following.
    1. **Clarify the investigation:** Identify the specific issue or phenomenon you are interested in.
    2. **Gather evidence:** Collect information relevant to the issue or phenomenon you are investigating. You could look at documents, conduct interviews, or make observations.
    3. **Interpret information:** Look for patterns, correlations, or anomalies in the evidence you collected. Use analytical tools and techniques as appropriate.
    4. **Formulate findings:** Summarize the key findings of your investigation and draw conclusions. What did the data reveal about your issue or phenomenon?

5. **Report results:** Create a report or presentation to communicate your findings, including the evidence that supports your conclusions.

COGNITIVE STRATEGY: **Systems Analysis**

PERFORMANCE LEVEL: **Utilization**

How to Incorporate It Into Classroom Practice:

- Teach students a process for systems analysis, such as the following.
    1. **Define the system:** Clearly describe the system you are analyzing, including its components, functions, and boundaries.
    2. **Gather data:** Compile information about the system's processes, requirements, and user needs. You can use interviews, surveys, observations, and existing documentation.
    3. **Map the system:** Create diagrams that represent the system's processes, how data flow through the system, and how parts of the system interact with each other.
    4. **Find opportunities to improve:** Identify inefficiencies or problems (gaps, redundancies, performance issues) in the system.
    5. **Develop solutions:** Recommend changes to the system that will eliminate inefficiencies or problems.

REFERENCES AND RESOURCES

Abbott, E. E. (1909). On the analysis of the factor of recall in the learning process. *The Psychological Review: Monograph Supplements*, *11*(1), 159–177. https://doi.org/10.1037/h0093018

Ackerman, R., & Thompson, V. A. (2017). Meta-reasoning: Monitoring and control of thinking and reasoning. *Trends in Cognitive Sciences*, *21*(8), 607–617. http://dx.doi.org/10.1016/j.tics.2017.05.004

Ackerman, R., & Thompson, V. A. (2018). Meta-reasoning: Shedding metacognitive light on reasoning research. In L. J. Ball & V. A. Thompson (Eds.), *The Routledge international handbook of thinking and reasoning* (pp. 1–15). Routledge. https://doi.org/10.4324/9781315725697

Adams, D. M., & Clark, D. B. (2014). Integrating self-explanation functionality into a complex game environment: Keeping gaming in motion. *Computers and Education*, *73*, 149–159. https://doi.org/10.1016/j.compedu.2014.01.002

Adesope, O. O., Trevisan, D. A., & Sundararajan, N. (2017). Rethinking the use of tests: A meta-analysis of practice testing. *Review of Educational Research*, *87*(3), 659–701. https://doi.org/10.3102/0034654316689306

Ainsworth, S., & Loizou, A. T. (2003). The effects of self-explaining when learning with text or diagrams. *Cognitive Science: A Multidisciplinary Journal*, *27*(4), 669–681. https://doi.org/10.1207/s15516709cog2704_5

Ambridge, B., Theakston, A. L., Lieven, E. V. M., & Tomasello, M. (2006). The distributed learning effect for children's acquisition of an abstract syntactic construction. *Cognitive Development*, *21*(2), 174–193. https://doi.org/10.1016/j.cogdev.2005.09.003

Anastasiou, D., Wirngo, C. N., & Bagos, P. (2024). The effectiveness of concept maps on students' achievement in science: A meta-analysis. *Educational Psychology Review*, *36*, Article 39. https://doi.org/10.1007/s10648-024-09877-y

Anderson, B. A. (2016a). The attention habit: How reward learning shapes attentional selection. *Annals of the New York Academy of Sciences*, *1369*(1), 24–39. https://doi.org/10.1111/nyas.12957

Anderson, B. A. (2016b). Social reward shapes attentional biases. *Cognitive Neuroscience*, *7*(1–4), 30–36. https://doi.org/10.1080/17588928.2015.1047823

Andrade, H. L., & Heritage, M. (2018). *Using formative assessment to enhance learning, achievement, and academic self-regulation*. Routledge. https://doi.org/10.4324/9781315623856

Azevedo, R., Taub, M., & Mudrick, N. V. (2018). Understanding and reasoning about real-time cognitive, affective, and metacognitive processes to foster self-regulation with advanced learning technologies. In D. H. Schunk & J. A. Greene (Eds.), *Handbook of self-regulation of learning and performance* (2nd ed., pp. 254–270). Routledge. https://doi.org/10.4324/9781315697048-17

Baars, M., Wijnia, L., de Bruin, A., & Paas, F. (2020). The relation between students' effort and monitoring judgments during learning: A meta-analysis. *Educational Psychology Review, 32*(4), 979–1002. https://doi.org/10.1007/s10648-020-09569-3

Baars, M., Wijnia, L., & Paas, F. (2017). The association between motivation, affect, and self-regulated learning when solving problems. *Frontiers in Psychology, 8*, Article 1346. https://doi.org/10.3389/fpsyg.2017.01346

Bacon, F. (2000). *The new organon* (M. Silverthorne, Trans.). Cambridge University Press. (Original work published 1620)

Badali, S., Rawson, K. A., & Dunlosky, J. (2023). How do students regulate their use of multiple choice practice tests? *Educational Psychology Review, 35*(2), Article 43. https://doi.org/10.1007/s10648-023-09761-1

Bandura, A. (1977). Self-efficacy: Toward a unifying theory of behavioral change. *Psychological Review, 84*(2), 191–215. https://doi.org/10.1037/0033-295X.84.2.191

Bandura, A. (1986). *Social foundations of thought and action: A social cognitive theory*. Prentice Hall.

Bandura, A. (1997). *Self-efficacy: The exercise of control*. W. H. Freeman.

Bandura, A. (2016). *Moral disengagement: How people do harm and live with themselves*. Worth.

Barta, A., Fodor, L. A., Tamas, B., & Szamoskozi, I. (2022). The development of students critical thinking abilities and dispositions through the concept mapping learning method—A meta-analysis. *Educational Research Review, 37*, Article 100481. https://doi.org/10.1016/j.edurev.2022.100481

Beuckels, E., Ye, G., Hudders, L., & Cauberghe, V. (2021). Media multitasking: A bibliometric approach and literature review. *Frontiers in Psychology, 12*, Article 623643. https://doi.org/10.3389/fpsyg.2021.623643

Blakeslee, S. (2004). The CRAAP Test. *LOEX Quarterly, 31*(3), Article 4. Accessed at https://commons.emich.edu/loexquarterly/vol31/iss3/4 on June 2, 2025.

Bloom, K. C., & Shuell, T. J. (1981). Effects of massed and distributed practice on the learning and retention of second-language vocabulary. *The Journal of Educational Research, 74*(4), 245–248. https://doi.org/10.1080/00220671.1981.10885317

Boekaerts, M. (2017). Cognitive load and self-regulation: Attempts to build a bridge. *Learning and Instruction, 51*, 90–97. http://dx.doi.org/10.1016/j.learninstruc.2017.07.001

Broadbent, D. E. (1958). *Perception and communication*. Pergamon Press. https://doi.org/10.1037/10037-000

Broadbent, J., & Poon, W. L. (2015). Self-regulated learning strategies & academic achievement in online higher education learning environments: A systematic review. *The Internet and Higher Education, 27*, 1–13. http://dx.doi.org/10.1016/j.iheduc.2015.04.007

Brookhart, S. M. (2018). Appropriate criteria: Key to effective rubrics. *Frontiers in Education, 3*, Article 22. https://doi.org/10.3389/feduc.2018.00022

Brookhart, S. M., & Chen, F. (2015). The quality and effectiveness of descriptive rubrics. *Educational Review, 67*(3), 343–368. https://doi.org/10.1080/00131911.2014.929565

Brooks, S. (2015). Does personal social media usage affect efficiency and well-being? *Computers in Human Behavior, 46*, 26–37. https://doi.org/10.1016/j.chb.2014.12.053

Brown, G. T. L., & Harris, L. R. (2013). Student self-assessment. In J. H. McMillan (Ed.), *SAGE handbook of research on classroom assessment* (pp. 367–393). SAGE.

Bureau, J. S., Howard, J. L., Chong, J. X. Y., & Guay, F. (2022). Pathways to student motivation: A meta-analysis of antecedents of autonomous and controlled motivations. *Review of Educational Research, 92*(1), 46–72. https://doi.org/10.3102/00346543211042426

Burns, E. C., Martin, A. J., & Collie, R. J. (2018). Adaptability, personal best (PB) goals setting, and gains in students' academic outcomes: A longitudinal examination from a social cognitive perspective. *Contemporary Educational Psychology, 53*, 57–72. https://doi.org/10.1016/j.cedpsych.2018.02.001

Butterfuss, R., & Kendeou, P. (2020). Reducing interference from misconceptions: The role of inhibition in knowledge revision. *Journal of Educational Psychology, 112*(4), 782–794. https://doi.org/10.1037/edu0000385

Cain, M. S., Leonard, J. A., Gabrieli, J. D. E., & Finn, A. S. (2016). Media multitasking in adolescence. *Psychonomic Bulletin and Review, 23*(6), 1932–1941. https://doi.org/10.3758/s13423-016-1036-3

Carlson, R. A., & Schneider, W. (1989). Acquisition context and the use of causal rules. *Memory and Cognition, 17*(3), 240–248. https://doi.org/10.3758/BF03198462

Carlson, R. A., & Yaure, R. G. (1990). Practice schedules and the use of component skills in problem solving. *Journal of Experimental Psychology: Learning, Memory, and Cognition, 16*(3), 484–496. https://doi.org/10.1037/0278-7393.16.3.484

Carpenter, S. K. (2023). Optimizing learning through retrieval practice and spacing. In R. J. Tierney, F. Rizvi, & K. Ercikan (Eds.), *International encyclopedia of education* (4th ed., pp. 664–672). Elsevier Science. https://doi.org/10.1016/B978-0-12-818630-5.14078-3

Carpenter, S. K., Lund, T. J. S., Coffman, C. R., Armstrong, P. I., Lamm, M. H., & Reason, R. D. (2016). A classroom study on the relationship between student achievement and retrieval-enhanced learning. *Educational Psychology Review, 28*(2), 353–375. https://doi.org/10.1007/s10648-015-9311-9

Carpenter, S. K., Pashler, H., & Cepeda, N. J. (2009). Using tests to enhance 8th grade students' retention of U.S. history facts. *Applied Cognitive Psychology, 23*(6), 760–771. https://doi.org/10.1002/acp.1507

Carvalho, P. F., & Goldstone, R. L. (2017). The sequence of study changes what information is attended to, encoded, and remembered during category learning. *Journal of Experimental Psychology: Learning, Memory, and Cognition, 43*(11), 1699–1719. https://doi.org/10.1037/xlm0000406

Carver, C. S., & Scheier, M. F. (2019). A self-regulatory viewpoint on human behavior. In R. M. Ryan (Ed.), *The Oxford handbook of human motivation* (2nd ed., pp. 27–46). Oxford University Press. https://doi.org/10.1093/oxfordhb/9780190666453.013.3

Chang, M., & Brainerd, C. J. (2022). Association and dissociation between judgments of learning and memory: A meta-analysis of the font size effect. *Metacognition and Learning, 17*(2), 443–476. https://doi.org/10.1007/s11409-021-09287-3

Chen, O., Paas, F., & Sweller, J. (2021). Spacing and interleaving effects require distinct theoretical bases: A systematic review testing the cognitive load and discriminative-contrast hypotheses. *Educational Psychology Review, 33*(4), 1499–1522. https://doi.org/10.1007/s10648-021-09613-w

Chi, M. T. H. (2021). The self-explanation principle in multimedia learning. In R. E. Mayer & L. Fiorella (Eds.), *The Cambridge handbook of multimedia learning* (3rd ed., pp. 381–393). Cambridge University Press. https://doi.org/10.1017/9781108894333.040

Chi, M. T. H., Bassok, M., Lewis, M. W., Reimann, P., & Glaser, R. (1989). Self-explanations: How students study and use examples in learning to solve problems. *Cognitive Science: A Multidisciplinary Journal, 13*(2), 145–182. https://doi.org/10.1207/s15516709cog1302_1

Chi, M. T. H., & VanLehn, K. A. (1991). The content of physics self-explanations. *Journal of the Learning Sciences, 1*(1), 69–105. https://doi.org/10.1207/s15327809jls0101_4

Chinn, C. A., & Duncan, R. G. (2021). Inquiry and learning. In R. G. Duncan & C. A. Chinn (Eds.), *International handbook of inquiry and learning* (pp. 1–14). Routledge. https://doi.org/10.4324/9781315685779

Costa, A. L., & Kallick, B. (Eds.). (2008). *Learning and leading with Habits of Mind: 16 essential characteristics for success.* ASCD.

Costa, A. L., & Kallick, B. (Eds.). (2009). *Habits of Mind across the curriculum: Practical and creative strategies for teachers.* ASCD.

Cross, E. S., Schmitt, P. J., & Grafton, S. T. (2007). Neural substrates of contextual interference during motor learning support a model of active preparation. *Journal of Cognitive Neuroscience, 19*(11), 1854–1871. https://doi.org/10.1162/jocn.2007.19.11.1854

Dawson, P. (2017). Assessment rubrics: Towards clearer and more replicable design, research and practice. *Assessment and Evaluation in Higher Education, 42*(3), 347–360. https://doi.org/10.1080/02602938.2015.1111294

de Boer, H., Donker, A. S., Kostons, D. D. N. M., & van der Werf, G. P. C. (2018). Long-term effects of metacognitive strategy instruction on student academic performance: A meta-analysis. *Educational Research Review, 24,* 98–115. https://doi.org/10.1016/j.edurev.2018.03.002

de Bruin, A. B. H., Kok, E. M., Lobbestael, J., & de Grip, A. (2017). The impact of an online tool for monitoring and regulating learning at university: Overconfidence, learning strategy, and personality. *Metacognition and Learning, 12*(1), 21–43. https://doi.org/10.1007/s11409-016-9159-5

de Bruin, A. B. H., Roelle, J., Carpenter, S. K., & Baars, M. (2020). Synthesizing cognitive load and self-regulation theory: A theoretical framework and research agenda. *Educational Psychology Review, 32,* 903–915. https://doi.org/10.1007/s10648-020-09576-4

de Croock, M. B. M., van Merriënboer, J. J. G., & Paas, F. G. W. C. (1998). High versus low contextual interference in simulation-based training of troubleshooting skills: Effects on transfer performance and invested mental effort. *Computers in Human Behavior, 14*(2), 249–267. https://doi.org/10.1016/S0747-5632(98)00005-3

De Koning, B. B., Tabbers, H. K., Rikers, R. M. J. P., & Paas, F. (2011). Improved effectiveness of cueing by self-explanations when learning from a complex animation. *Applied Cognitive Psychology, 25*(2), 183–194. https://doi.org/10.1002/acp.1661

de Ruig, N. J., de Jong, P. F., & Zee, M. (2023). Stimulating elementary school students' self-regulated learning through high-quality interactions and relationships: A narrative review. *Educational Psychology Review, 35*(3), Article 71. https://doi.org/10.1007/s10648-023-09795-5

Deci, E. L., & Ryan, R. M. (1987). The support of autonomy and the control of behavior. *Journal of Personality and Social Psychology, 53*(6), 1024–1037. https://doi.org/10.1037/0022-3514.53.6.1024

Deci, E. L., & Ryan, R. M. (2000). The "what" and "why" of goal pursuits: Human needs and the self-determination of behavior. *Psychological Inquiry, 11*(4), 227–268. https://doi.org/10.1207/S15327965PLI1104_01

Deci, E. L., & Ryan, R. M. (2012). Motivation, personality, and development within embedded social contexts: An overview of self-determination theory. In R. M. Ryan (Ed.), *The Oxford handbook of human motivation* (pp. 85–108). Oxford University Press. https://doi.org/10.1093/oxfordhb/9780195399820.013.0006

Deekens, V. M., Greene, J. A., & Lobczowski, N. G. (2018). Monitoring and depth of strategy use in computer-based learning environments for science and history. *British Journal of Educational Psychology, 88*(1), 63–79. https://doi.org/10.1111/bjep.12174

Dent, A. L., & Koenka, A. C. (2016). The relation between self-regulated learning and academic achievement across childhood and adolescence: A meta-analysis. *Educational Psychology Review, 28*(3), 425–474. https://doi.org/10.1007/s10648-015-9320-8

Destan, N., Hembacher, E., Ghetti, S., & Roebers, C. M. (2014). Early metacognitive abilities: The interplay of monitoring and control processes in 5- to 7-year-old children. *Journal of Experimental Child Psychology, 126*, 213–228. https://doi.org/10.1016/j.jecp.2014.04.001

Destan, N., & Roebers, C. M. (2015). What are the metacognitive costs of young children's overconfidence? *Metacognition and Learning, 10*(3), 347–374. https://doi.org/10.1007/s11409-014-9133-z

Diamond, A. (2013). Executive functions. *Annual Review of Psychology, 64*, 135–168. https://doi.org/10.1146/annurev-psych-113011-143750

Diamond, A. (2016). Why improving and assessing executive functions early in life is critical. In J. A. Griffin, P. McCardle, & L. S. Freund (Eds.), *Executive function in preschool-age children: Integrating measurement, neurodevelopment, and translational research* (pp. 11–43). American Psychological Association. https://doi.org/10.1037/14797-002

Diana, N. (2020). *Value-adaptive instruction: Improving the productivity of civil discourse and addressing bias* [Doctoral dissertation, Carnegie Mellon University]. KiltHub @ Carnegie Mellon University. https://kilthub.cmu.edu/articles/thesis/Value-Adaptive_Instruction_Improving_the_Productivity_of_Civil_Discourse_and_Addressing_Bias/13862879?file=26425670

Dignath, C., Buettner, G., & Langfeldt, H.-P. (2008). How can primary school students learn self-regulated learning strategies most effectively? A meta-analysis on self-regulation training programmes. *Educational Research Review, 3*(2), 101–129. https://doi.org/10.1016/j.edurev.2008.02.003

Dignath, C., & Büttner, G. (2008). Components of fostering self-regulated learning among students. A meta-analysis on intervention studies at primary and secondary school level. *Metacognition and Learning, 3*(3), 231–264. https://doi.org/10.1007/s11409-008-9029-x

Dignath, C., van Ewijk, R., Perels, F., & Fabriz, S. (2023). Let learners monitor the learning content and their learning behavior! A meta-analysis on the effectiveness of tools to foster monitoring. *Educational Psychology Review, 35*(2), Article 62. https://doi.org/10.1007/s10648-023-09718-4

Dignath, C., & Veenman, M. V. J. (2021). The role of direct strategy instruction and indirect activation of self-regulated learning—Evidence from classroom observation studies. *Educational Psychology Review, 33*(2), 489–533. https://doi.org/10.1007/s10648-020-09534-0

Dobson, J. L., Perez, J., & Linderholm, T. (2017). Distributed retrieval practice promotes superior recall of anatomy information. *Anatomical Sciences Education, 10*(4), 339–347. https://doi.org/10.1002/ase.1668

Donker, A. S., de Boer, H., Kostons, D., Dignath van Ewijk, C. C., & van der Werf, M. P. C. (2014). Effectiveness of learning strategy instruction on academic performance: A meta-analysis. *Educational Research Review, 11*, 1–26. https://doi.org/10.1016/j.edurev.2013.11.002

Dönmez, O., & Akbulut, Y. (2021). Timing and relevance of secondary tasks impact multitasking performance. *Computers and Education, 161*, Article 104078. https://doi.org/10.1016/j.compedu.2020.104078

Donoghue, G. M., & Hattie, J. A. C. (2021). A meta-analysis of ten learning techniques. *Frontiers in Education, 6*, Article 581216. https://doi.org/10.3389/feduc.2021.581216

Ebbinghaus, H. (1913). *Memory: A contribution to experimental psychology* (H. A. Ruger & C. E. Bussenius, Trans.). Teachers College Press. (Original work published 1885)

Ebersbach, M., Feierabend, M., & Nazari, K. B. B. (2020). Comparing the effects of generating questions, testing, and restudying on students' long-term recall in university learning. *Applied Cognitive Psychology, 34*(3), 724–736. https://doi.org/10.1002/acp.3639

Eccles, J. S., & Wigfield, A. (2020). From expectancy-value theory to situated expectancy-value theory: A developmental, social cognitive, and sociocultural perspective on motivation. *Contemporary Educational Psychology, 61*, Article 101859. https://doi.org/10.1016/j.cedpsych.2020.101859

Efklides, A., Schwartz, B. L., & Brown, V. (2018). Motivation and affect in self-regulated learning: Does metacognition play a role? In D. H. Schunk & J. A. Greene (Eds.), *Handbook of self-regulation of learning and performance* (2nd ed., pp. 64–82). Routledge. https://doi.org/10.4324/9781315697048-5

Eglington, L. G., & Kang, S. H. K. (2017). Interleaved presentation benefits science category learning. *Journal of Applied Research in Memory and Cognition, 6*(4), 475–485. https://doi.org/10.1016/j.jarmac.2017.07.005

Elhusseini, S. A., Tischner, C. M., Aspiranti, K. B., & Fedewa, A. L. (2022). A quantitative review of the effects of self-regulation interventions on primary and secondary student academic achievement. *Metacognition and Learning, 17*(3), 1117–1139. https://doi.org/10.1007/s11409-022-09311-0

Elliot, A. J., & Sommet, N. (2023). Integration in the achievement motivation literature and the hierarchical model of achievement motivation. *Educational Psychology Review, 35*(3), Article 77. https://doi.org/10.1007/s10648-023-09785-7

English, T., Lee, I. A., John, O. P., & Gross, J. J. (2017). Emotion regulation strategy selection in daily life: The role of social context and goals. *Motivation and Emotion, 41*(2), 230–242. https://doi.org/10.1007/s11031-016-9597-z

Ennis, R., Millman, J., & Tomko, T. N. (2005). *Cornell critical thinking tests, levels X and Z: Administration manual* (5th ed.). Critical Thinking.

Ericsson, K. A., & Harwell, K. W. (2019). Deliberate practice and proposed limits on the effects of practice on the acquisition of expert performance: Why the original definition matters and recommendations for future research. *Frontiers in Psychology, 10,* Article 2396. https://doi.org/10.3389/fpsyg.2019.02396

Eshuis, E. H., ter Vrugte, J., & de Jong, T. (2022). Supporting reflection to improve learning from self-generated concept maps. *Metacognition and Learning, 17*(3), 691–713. https://doi.org/10.1007/s11409-022-09299-7

Evans, J. S. B. T. (2019). Deductive reasoning. In R. J. Sternberg & J. Funke (Eds.), *The psychology of human thought: An introduction* (pp. 113–132). Heidelberg University. https://doi.org/10.17885/heiup.470

Fiedler, K., Ackerman, R., & Scarampi, C. (2019). Metacognition: Monitoring and controlling one's own knowledge, reasoning and decisions. In R. J. Sternberg & J. Funke (Eds.), *The psychology of human thought: An introduction* (pp. 89–111). Heidelberg University. https://doi.org/10.17885/heiup.470

Fiorella, L. (2020). The science of habit and its implications for student learning and well-being. *Educational Psychology Review, 32*(3), 603–625. https://doi.org/10.1007/s10648-020-09525-1

Fiorella, L., & Kuhlmann, S. (2020). Creating drawings enhances learning by teaching. *Journal of Educational Psychology, 112*(4), 811–822. https://doi.org/10.1037/edu0000392

Fiorella, L., & Mayer, R. E. (2013). The relative benefits of learning by teaching and teaching expectancy. *Contemporary Educational Psychology, 38*(4), 281–288. https://doi.org/10.1016/j.cedpsych.2013.06.001

Fiorella, L., Stull, A. T., Kuhlmann, S., & Mayer, R. E. (2020). Fostering generative learning from video lessons: Benefits of instructor-generated drawings and learner-generated explanations. *Journal of Educational Psychology, 112*(5), 895–906. https://doi.org/10.1037/edu0000408

Firth, J., Rivers, I., & Boyle, J. (2021). A systematic review of interleaving as a concept learning strategy. *Review of Education, 9*(2), 642–684. https://doi.org/10.1002/rev3.3266

Fischer, F., Kollar, I., Ufer, S., Sodian, B., Hussmann, H., Pekrun, R., et al. (2014). Scientific reasoning and argumentation: Advancing an interdisciplinary research agenda in education. *Frontline Learning Research, 2*(3), 28–45. https://doi.org/10.14786/flr.v2i2.96

Fitch, M. L., Drucker, A. J., & Norton, J. A., Jr. (1951). Frequent testing as a motivating factor in large lecture classes. *Journal of Educational Psychology, 42*(1), 1–20. https://doi.org/10.1037/h0056095

Flavell, J. H. (1979). Metacognition and cognitive monitoring: A new area of cognitive–developmental inquiry. *American Psychologist, 34*(10), 906–911. https://doi.org/10.1037/0003-066X.34.10.906

Forsblom, L., Pekrun, R., Loderer, K., & Peixoto, F. (2022). Cognitive appraisals, achievement emotions, and students' math achievement: A longitudinal analysis. *Journal of Educational Psychology, 114*(2), 346–367. https://doi.org/10.1037/edu0000671

Foster, N. L., Rawson, K. A., & Dunlosky, J. (2018). Self-regulated learning of principle-based concepts: Do students prefer worked examples, faded examples, or problem solving? *Learning and Instruction, 55,* 124–138. https://doi.org/10.1016/j.learninstruc.2017.10.002

Fréchette-Simard, C., Plante, I., Duchesne, S., & Chaffee, K. E. (2022). The mediating role of test anxiety in the evolution of motivation and achievement of students transitioning from elementary to high school. *Contemporary Educational Psychology, 71*, Article 102116. https://doi.org/10.1016/j.cedpsych.2022.102116

Gagné, E. D., Yekovich, C. W., & Yekovich, F. R. (1993). *The cognitive psychology of school learning* (2nd ed.). HarperCollins College.

Gates, A. I. (1917). *Recitation as a factor in memorizing* [Doctoral dissertation, Columbia University]. Internet Archive. Accessed at https://dn790007.ca.archive.org/0/items/recitationasfact00gaterich/recitationasfact00gaterich.pdf on June 2, 2025.

Gergen, K. J. (2015). *An invitation to social construction* (3rd ed.). SAGE.

Geurten, M., & Bastin, C. (2019). Behaviors speak louder than explicit reports: Implicit metacognition in 2.5-year-old children. *Developmental Science, 22*(2), Article e12742. https://doi.org/10.1111/desc.12742

Giunchiglia, F., Zeni, M., Gobbi, E., Bignotti, E., & Bison, I. (2018). Mobile social media usage and academic performance. *Computers in Human Behavior, 82*, 177–185. https://doi.org/10.1016/j.chb.2017.12.041

Goetz, T., Frenzel, A. C., Stockinger, K., Lipnevich, A. A., Stempfer, L., & Pekrun, R. (2023). Emotions in education. In R. J. Tierney, F. Rizvi, & K. Ercikan (Eds.), *International encyclopedia of education* (4th ed., pp. 149–161). Elsevier Science. https://doi.org/10.1016/B978-0-12-818630-5.14032-1

Goossens, N. A. M. C., Camp, G., Verkoeijen, P. P. J. L., & Tabbers, H. K. (2014). The effect of retrieval practice in primary school vocabulary learning. *Applied Cognitive Psychology, 28*(1), 135–142. https://doi.org/10.1002/acp.2956

Graham, S., Hebert, M., & Harris, K. R. (2015). Formative assessment and writing: A meta-analysis. *The Elementary School Journal, 115*(4), 523–547. https://doi.org/10.1086/681947

Greene, J. A. (2018). *Self-regulation in education.* Routledge.

Greene, J. A. (2021). Teacher support for metacognition and self-regulated learning: A compelling story and a prototypical model. *Metacognition and Learning, 16*(3), 651–666. https://doi.org/10.1007/s11409-021-09283-7

Greene, J. A., Bolick, C. M., Caprino, A. M., Deekens, V. M., McVea, M., Yu, S., et al. (2015). Fostering high-school students' self-regulated learning online and across academic domains. *The High School Journal, 99*(1), 88–106. https://doi.org/10.1353/hsj.2015.0019

Greene, J. A., Sandoval, W. A., & Bråten, I. (Eds.). (2016). *Handbook of epistemic cognition.* Routledge.

Guadagnoli, M. A., & Lee, T. D. (2004). Challenge point: A framework for conceptualizing the effects of various practice conditions in motor learning. *Journal of Motor Behavior, 36*(2), 212–224. https://doi.org/10.3200/JMBR.36.2.212-224

Gutierrez de Blume, A. P. (2022). Calibrating calibration: A meta-analysis of learning strategy instruction interventions to improve metacognitive monitoring accuracy. *Journal of Educational Psychology, 114*(4), 681–700. https://doi.org/10.1037/edu0000674

Guzman, G., Goldberg, T. S., & Swanson, H. L. (2018). A meta-analysis of self-monitoring on reading performance of K–12 students. *School Psychology Quarterly, 33*(1), 160–168. https://doi.org/10.1037/spq0000199

Hadwin, A. (2021). Commentary and future directions: What can multi-modal data reveal about temporal and adaptive processes in self-regulated learning? *Learning and Instruction, 72*, Article 101287. https://doi.org/10.1016/j.learninstruc.2019.101287

Hadwin, A., Järvelä, S., & Miller, M. (2018). Self-regulation, co-regulation, and shared regulation in collaborative learning environments. In D. H. Schunk & J. A. Greene (Eds.), *Handbook of self-regulation of learning and performance* (2nd ed., pp. 83–106). Routledge. https://doi.org /10.4324/9781315697048-6

Halloun, I. A. (2023). *Systemic cognition and education: Empowering students for excellence in life*. Springer.

Hamm, J. M., Tan, J. X. Y., Barlow, M. A., Delaney, R. L., & Duggan, K. A. (2022). Goal adjustment capacities in uncontrollable life circumstances: Benefits for psychological well-being during COVID-19. *Motivation and Emotion, 46*(3), 319–335. https://doi.org/10.1007/s11031-022-09941-6

Hart, J. T. (1965). Memory and the feeling-of-knowing experience. *Journal of Educational Psychology, 56*(4), 208–216. https://doi.org/10.1037/h0022263

Hart, J. T. (1967). Memory and the memory-monitoring process. *Journal of Verbal Learning and Verbal Behavior, 6*(5), 685–691. https://doi.org/10.1016/S0022-5371(67)80072-0

Hattie, J., Biggs, J., & Purdie, N. (1996). Effects of learning skills interventions on student learning: A meta-analysis. *Review of Educational Research, 66*(2), 99–136. https://doi.org/10.3102 /00346543066002099

Hays, M. J., Kornell, N., & Bjork, R. A. (2013). When and why a failed test potentiates the effectiveness of subsequent study. *Journal of Experimental Psychology: Learning, Memory, and Cognition, 39*(1), 290–296. https://doi.org/10.1037/a0028468

Helsdingen, A. S., van Gog, T., & van Merriënboer, J. J. G. (2011). The effects of practice schedule on learning a complex judgment task. *Learning and Instruction, 21*(1), 126–136. https://doi.org /10.1016/j.learninstruc.2009.12.001

Heuristic. (n.d.). In *Cambridge Dictionary's online dictionary*. Accessed at https://dictionary. cambridge.org/us/dictionary/english/heuristic on November 1, 2024.

Hidi, S. (2016). Revisiting the role of rewards in motivation and learning: Implications of neuroscientific research. *Educational Psychology Review, 28*(1), 61–93. https://doi.org/10.1007/s10648-015 -9307-5

Hillegas, M. B. (1912). A scale for the measurement of quality in English composition by young people. *Teachers College Record, 13*(4). https://doi.org/10.1177/016146811201300411

Hoch, E., Sidi, Y., Ackerman, R., Hoogerheide, V., & Scheiter, K. (2023). Comparing mental effort, difficulty, and confidence appraisals in problem-solving: A metacognitive perspective. *Educational Psychology Review, 35*(2), Article 61. https://doi.org/10.1007/s10648-023-09779-5

Hopkins, R. F., Lyle, K. B., Hieb, J. L., & Ralston, P. A. S. (2016). Spaced retrieval practice increases college students' short- and long-term retention of mathematics knowledge. *Educational Psychology Review, 28*(4), 853–873. https://doi.org/10.1007/s10648-015-9349-8

Hornstra, L., Stroet, K., Rubie-Davies, C., & Flint, A. (2023). Teacher expectations and self-determination theory: Considering convergence and divergence of theories. *Educational Psychology Review, 35*(3), Article 76. https://doi.org/10.1007/s10648-023-09788-4

Howard, J. L., Bureau, J., Guay, F., Chong, J. X. Y., & Ryan, R. M. (2021). Student motivation and associated outcomes: A meta-analysis from self-determination theory. *Perspectives on Psychological Science, 16*(6), 1300–1323. https://doi.org/10.1177/1745691620966789

Hoyle, R. H., & Dent, A. L. (2018). Developmental trajectories of skills and abilities relevant for self-regulation of learning and performance. In D. H. Schunk & J. A. Greene (Eds.), *Handbook of self-regulation of learning and performance* (2nd ed., pp. 49–63). Routledge. https://doi.org/10.4324/9781315697048-4

Hulbig, P. R. (2023). *The pedagogy of self-authorship: The neurocognitive impact of science and metacognition.* Springer.

Inzlicht, M., Werner, K. M., Briskin, J. L., & Roberts, B. W. (2021). Integrating models of self-regulation. *Annual Review of Psychology, 72,* 319–345. https://doi.org/10.1146/annurev-psych-061020-105721

Iordanou, K. (2022). Supporting strategic and meta-strategic development of argument skill: The role of reflection. *Metacognition and Learning, 17*(2), 399–425. https://doi.org/10.1007/s11409-021-09289-1

Jacoby, L. L. (1978). On interpreting the effects of repetition: Solving a problem versus remembering a solution. *Journal of Verbal Learning and Verbal Behavior, 17*(6), 649–667. https://doi.org/10.1016/S0022-5371(78)90393-6

Jaeger, A., Eisenkraemer, R. E., & Stein, L. M. (2015). Test-enhanced learning in third-grade children. *Educational Psychology, 35*(4), 513–521. https://doi.org/10.1080/01443410.2014.963030

James, W. (1890). *The principles of psychology.* Holt.

Jansen, R. S., van Leeuwen, A., Janssen, J., Jak, S., & Kester, L. (2019). Self-regulated learning partially mediates the effect of self-regulated learning interventions on achievement in higher education: A meta-analysis. *Educational Research Review, 28,* Article 100292. https://doi.org/10.1016/j.edurev.2019.100292

Janssen, E. M., van Gog, T., van de Groep, L., de Lange, A. J., Knopper, R. L., Onan, E., et al. (2023). The role of mental effort in students' perceptions of the effectiveness of interleaved and blocked study strategies and their willingness to use them. *Educational Psychology Review, 35*(3), Article 85. https://doi.org/10.1007/s10648-023-09797-3

Jones, A. C., Wardlow, L., Pan, S. C., Zepeda, C., Heyman, G. D., Dunlosky, J., et al. (2016). Beyond the rainbow: Retrieval practice leads to better spelling than does rainbow writing. *Educational Psychology Review, 28*(2), 385–400. https://doi.org/10.1007/s10648-015-9330-6

Jonsson, A., & Svingby, G. (2007). The use of scoring rubrics: Reliability, validity and educational consequences. *Educational Research Review, 2*(2), 130–144. https://doi.org/10.1016/j.edurev.2007.05.002

Junco, R., & Cotten, S. R. (2012). No A 4 U: The relationship between multitasking and academic performance. *Computers and Education, 59*(2), 505–514. https://doi.org/10.1016/j.compedu.2011.12.023

Kälin, S., & Roebers, C. M. (2022). Longitudinal associations between executive functions and metacognitive monitoring in 5- to 8-year-olds. *Metacognition and Learning, 17*(3), 1079–1095. https://doi.org/10.1007/s11409-022-09306-x

Kallick, B., & Zmuda, A. (2017). *Students at the center: Personalized learning with Habits of Mind.* ASCD.

Kaminske, A., Brown, A., Aylward, A., & Haller, M. (2022). Cell phone notifications harm attention: An exploration of the factors that contribute to distraction. *European Journal of Educational Research, 11*(3), 1487–1494. https://doi.org/10.12973/eu-jer.11.3.1487

Kapur, M. (2014). Comparing learning from productive failure and vicarious failure. *Journal of the Learning Sciences, 23*(4), 651–677. https://doi.org/10.1080/10508406.2013.819000

Kapur, M. (2016). Examining productive failure, productive success, unproductive failure, and unproductive success in learning. *Educational Psychologist, 51*(2), 289–299. https://doi.org/10.1080/00461520.2016.1155457

Kim, Y., Yu, S. L., Wolters, C. A., & Anderman, E. M. (2023). Self-regulatory processes within and between diverse goals: The multiple goals regulation framework. *Educational Psychologist, 58*(2), 70–91. https://doi.org/10.1080/00461520.2022.2158828

Kinchin, I. M. (2014). Concept mapping as a learning tool in higher education: A critical analysis of recent reviews. *The Journal of Continuing Higher Education, 62*(1), 39–49. https://doi.org/10.1080/07377363.2014.872011

Kirk-Johnson, A., Galla, B. M., & Fraundorf, S. H. (2019). Perceiving effort as poor learning: The misinterpreted-effort hypothesis of how experienced effort and perceived learning relate to study strategy choice. *Cognitive Psychology, 115*, Article 101237. https://doi.org/10.1016/j.cogpsych.2019.101237

Kohn, A. (2006). Speaking my mind: The trouble with rubrics. *English Journal, 95*(4), 12–15. https://doi.org/10.2307/30047080

Kong, F., Meng, S., Deng, H., Wang, M., & Sun, X. (2023). Cognitive control in adolescents and young adults with media multitasking experience: A three-level meta-analysis. *Educational Psychology Review, 35*(1), Article 22. https://doi.org/10.1007/s10648-023-09746-0

Kornell, N., Hays, M. J., & Bjork, R. A. (2009). Unsuccessful retrieval attempts enhance subsequent learning. *Journal of Experimental Psychology: Learning, Memory, and Cognition, 35*(4), 989–998. https://doi.org/10.1037/a0015729

Krieger, F., Azevedo, R., Graesser, A. C., & Greiff, S. (2022). Introduction to the special issue: The role of metacognition in complex skills—Spotlights on problem solving, collaboration, and self-regulated learning. *Metacognition and Learning, 17*(3), 683–690. https://doi.org/10.1007/s11409-022-09327-6

Kubik, V., Jemstedt, A., Eshratabadi, H. M., Schwartz, B. L., & Jönsson, F. U. (2022). The underconfidence-with-practice effect in action memory: The contribution of retrieval practice to metacognitive monitoring. *Metacognition and Learning, 17*(2), 375–398. https://doi.org/10.1007/s11409-021-09288-2

Kuhn, D. (2019). Critical thinking as discourse. *Human Development, 62*(3), 146–164. https://doi.org/10.1159/000500171

Kuhn, D. (2020). Why is reconciling divergent views a challenge? *Current Directions in Psychological Science, 29*(1), 27–32. https://doi.org/10.1177/0963721419885996

Kuhn, D. (2022). Metacognition matters in many ways. *Educational Psychologist, 57*(2), 73–86. https://doi.org/10.1080/00461520.2021.1988603

Kuhn, D., & Modrek, A. (2018). Do reasoning limitations undermine discourse? *Thinking and Reasoning, 24*(1), 97–116. https://doi.org/10.1080/13546783.2017.1388846

Lachner, A., Ly, K.-T., & Nückles, M. (2018). Providing written or oral explanations? Differential effects of the modality of explaining on students' conceptual learning and transfer. *The Journal of Experimental Education, 86*(3), 344–361. http://dx.doi.org/10.1080/00220973.2017.1363691

Laursen, S. J., & Fiacconi, C. M. (2022). Constraints on the use of the memorizing effort heuristic. *Metacognition and Learning, 17*(1), 1–51. https://doi.org/10.1007/s11409-021-09273-9

Lazonder, A. W., & Harmsen, R. (2016). Meta-analysis of inquiry-based learning: Effects of guidance. *Review of Educational Research, 86*(3), 681–718. https://doi.org/10.3102/0034654315627366

Lee, H. J., & Bong, M. (2023). Self-efficacy. In R. J. Tierney, F. Rizvi, & K. Ercikan (Eds.), *International encyclopedia of education* (4th ed., pp. 250–257). Elsevier Science. https://doi.org/10.1016/B978-0-12-818630-5.14028-X

Leslie, A. M. (1987). Pretense and representation: The origins of "theory of mind." *Psychological Review, 94*(4), 412–426. https://doi.org/10.1037/0033-295X.94.4.412

Levesque-Bristol, C., Richards, K. A. R., Zissimopoulos, A., Wang, C., & Yu, S. (2022). An evaluation of the integrative model for learning and motivation in the college classroom. *Current Psychology, 41*(3), 1447–1459. https://doi.org/10.1007/s12144-020-00671-x

Li, J., Ye, H., Tang, Y., Zhou, Z., & Hu, X. (2018). What are the effects of self-regulation phases and strategies for Chinese students? A meta-analysis of two decades research of the association between self-regulation and academic performance. *Frontiers in Psychology, 9*, Article 2434. https://doi.org/10.3389/fpsyg.2018.02434

Li, L.-Y. (2019). Effect of prior knowledge on attitudes, behavior, and learning performance in video lecture viewing. *International Journal of Human–Computer Interaction, 35*(4–5), 415–426. https://doi.org/10.1080/10447318.2018.1543086

Li, Y., Raković, M., Dai, W., Lin, J., Khosravi, H., Galbraith, K., et al. (2023). Are deeper reflectors better goal-setters? AI-empowered analytics of reflective writing in pharmaceutical education. *Computers and Education: Artificial Intelligence, 5*, Article 100157. https://doi.org/10.1016/j.caeai.2023.100157

Liem, G. A. D., & Senko, C. (2022). Goal complexes: A new approach to studying the coordination, consequences, and social contexts of pursuing multiple goals. *Educational Psychology Review, 34*(4), 2167–2195. https://doi.org/10.1007/s10648-022-09701-5

Linnenbrink-Garcia, L., Patall, E. A., & Pekrun, R. (2016). Adaptive motivation and emotion in education: Research and principles for instructional design. *Policy Insights From the Behavioral and Brain Sciences, 3*(2), 228–236. https://doi.org/10.1177/2372732216644450

Locke, E. A., & Latham, G. P. (2002). Building a practically useful theory of goal setting and task motivation: A 35-year odyssey. *American Psychologist, 57*(9), 705–717. https://doi.org/10.1037/0003-066X.57.9.705

Locke, E. A., & Latham, G. P. (2013). Goal setting theory: The current state. In E. A. Locke & G. P. Latham (Eds.), *New developments in goal setting and task performance* (pp. 623–630). Routledge. https://doi.org/10.4324/9780203082744

Lyons, K. E., & Ghetti, S. (2011). The development of uncertainty monitoring in early childhood. *Child Development, 82*(6), 1778–1787. https://doi.org/10.1111/j.1467-8624.2011.01649.x

Macagno, F. (2016). Argument relevance and structure. Assessing and developing students' uses of evidence. *International Journal of Educational Research, 79*, 180–194. https://doi.org/10.1016/j.ijer.2016.07.002

Macagno, F., & Walton, D. (2018). Practical reasoning arguments: A modular approach. *Argumentation, 32*(4), 519–547. https://doi.org/10.1007/s10503-018-9450-5

Magill, R. A., & Hall, K. G. (1990). A review of the contextual interference effect in motor skill acquisition. *Human Movement Science, 9*(3–5), 241–289. https://doi.org/10.1016/0167-9457(90)90005-X

Mark, G., Czerwinski, M., & Iqbal, S. T. (2018, April 21–26). Effects of individual differences in blocking workplace distractions [Paper No. 92]. *CHI 2018: Proceedings of the 2018 CHI Conference on Human Factors in Computing Systems*. Association for Computing Machinery. https://doi.org/10.1145/3173574.3173666

Martin, A. J., Burns, E. C., Collie, R. J., Bostwick, K. C. P., Flesken, A., & McCarthy, I. (2022). Growth goal setting in high school: A large-scale study of perceived instructional support, personal background attributes, and engagement outcomes. *Journal of Educational Psychology, 114*(4), 752–771. https://doi.org/10.1037/edu0000682

Marzano, R. J. (1992). *A different kind of classroom: Teaching with Dimensions of Learning*. ASCD.

Marzano, R. J. (2000). *Transforming classroom grading*. ASCD.

Marzano, R. J. (2007). *The art and science of teaching: A comprehensive framework for effective instruction*. ASCD.

Marzano, R. J. (2019). *Understanding rigor in the classroom*. Learning Sciences International.

Marzano, R. J., & Abbott, S. D. (2022). *Teaching in a competency-based elementary school: The Marzano Academies model*. Marzano Resources.

Marzano, R. J., & Arredondo, D. E. (1986). *Tactics for thinking: Teacher's manual*. ASCD.

Marzano, R. J., Brandt, R. S., Hughes, C. S., Jones, B. F., Presseisen, B. Z., Rankin, S. C., et al. (1988). *Dimensions of thinking: A framework for curriculum and instruction*. ASCD.

Marzano, R. J., & Heflebower, T. (2012). *Teaching & assessing 21st century skills*. Marzano Resources.

Marzano, R. J., & Kendall, J. S. (1996). *A comprehensive guide to designing standards-based districts, schools, and classrooms*. ASCD.

Marzano, R. J., & Kendall, J. S. (1998). *Implementing standards-based education*. National Education Association.

Marzano, R. J., & Kosena, B. J. (2022). *Leading a competency-based elementary school: The Marzano Academies model*. Marzano Resources.

Marzano, R. J., Norford, J. S., Finn, M., & Finn, D., III. (2017). *A handbook for personalized competency-based education*. Marzano Resources.

Marzano, R. J., & Pickering, D. J. (1997). *Dimensions of Learning: Teacher's manual* (2nd ed.). ASCD.

Marzano, R. J., Pickering, D. J., & Pollock, J. E. (2001). *Classroom instruction that works: Research-based strategies for increasing student achievement*. ASCD.

Matos, L., Reeve, J., Herrera, D., & Claux, M. (2018). Students' agentic engagement predicts longitudinal increases in perceived autonomy-supportive teaching: The squeaky wheel gets the grease. *The Journal of Experimental Education, 86*(4), 579–596. https://doi.org/10.1080/00220973.2018.1448746

Mayer, R. E. (2023). Problem solving. In R. J. Tierney, F. Rizvi, & K. Ercikan (Eds.), *International encyclopedia of education* (4th ed., pp. 229–234). Elsevier Science. https://doi.org/10.1016/B978-0-12-818630-5.14023-0

McCarthy, K. S., & McNamara, D. S. (2023). Knowledge: A fundamental asset. In R. J. Tierney, F. Rizvi, & K. Ercikan (Eds.), *International encyclopedia of education* (4th ed., pp. 209–218). Elsevier Science. https://doi.org/10.1016/B978-0-12-818630-5.14016-3

McClelland, M. M., Ahmadi, A., & Wanless, S. B. (2023). Self-regulation. In H. S. Friedman & C. H. Markey (Eds.), *Encyclopedia of mental health* (3rd ed., pp. 176–184). Academic Press. https://doi.org/10.1016/B978-0-323-91497-0.00042-4

McClelland, M. M., Tominey, S. L., Schmitt, S. A., Hatfield, B. E., Purpura, D. J., Gonzales, C. R., et al. (2019). Red light, purple light! Results of an intervention to promote school readiness for children from low-income backgrounds. *Frontiers in Psychology, 10,* Article 2365. https://doi.org/10.3389/fpsyg.2019.02365

McDermott, K. B., Agarwal, P. K., D'Antonio, L., Roediger, H. L., III, & McDaniel, M. A. (2014). Both multiple-choice and short-answer quizzes enhance later exam performance in middle and high school classes. *Journal of Experimental Psychology: Applied, 20*(1), 3–21. https://doi.org/10.1037/xap0000004

McGuinness, C. (1999, April). *From thinking skills to thinking classrooms: A review and evaluation of approaches for developing pupils' thinking* (Department for Education and Employment Research Report No. 115). Crown Copyright. Accessed at www.researchgate.net/profile/Carol-Mcguinness/publication/280100115_From_Thinking_Skills_to_Thinking_Classrooms_A_review_and_evaluation_of_approaches_for_developing_pupils'_thinking/links/55a9319f08aea3d0868033e8/From-Thinking-Skills-to-Thinking-Classrooms-A-review-and-evaluation-of-approaches-for-developing-pupils-thinking.pdf on April 2, 2025.

Mera, Y., Rodríguez, G., & Marin-Garcia, E. (2022). Unraveling the benefits of experiencing errors during learning: Definition, modulating factors, and explanatory theories. *Psychonomic Bulletin and Review, 29*(3), 753–765. https://doi.org/10.3758/s13423-021-02022-8

Metcalfe, J. (2017). Learning from errors. *Annual Review of Psychology, 68,* 465–489. https://doi.org/10.1146/annurev-psych-010416-044022

Metcalfe, J., & Xu, J. (2018). Learning from one's own errors and those of others. *Psychonomic Bulletin and Review, 25*(1), 402–408. https://doi.org/10.3758/s13423-017-1287-7

Milner, A. E., MacLean, M. H., & Giesbrecht, B. (2023). The persistence of value-driven attention capture is task-dependent. *Attention, Perception, and Psychophysics, 85*(2), 315–341. https://doi.org/10.3758/s13414-022-02621-0

Mitchell, T. R., Harman, W. S., Lee, T. W., & Lee, D.-Y. (2008). Self-regulation and multiple deadline goals. In R. Kanfer, G. Chen, & R. D. Pritchard (Eds.), *Work motivation: Past, present, and future* (pp. 197–231). Routledge.

Moos, D. C. (2018). Emerging classroom technology: Using self-regulation principles as a guide for effective implementation. In D. H. Schunk & J. A. Greene (Eds.), *Handbook of self-regulation of learning and performance* (2nd ed., pp. 243–253). Routledge. https://doi.org/10.4324/9781315697048-16

Moshman, D. (2015). *Epistemic cognition and development: The psychology of justification and truth.* Psychology Press.

Muncer, G., Higham, P. A., Gosling, C. J., Cortese, S., Wood-Downie, H., & Hadwin, J. A. (2022). A meta-analysis investigating the association between metacognition and math performance in adolescence. *Educational Psychology Review, 34*(1), 301–334. https://doi.org/10.1007/s10648-021-09620-x

National Governors Association Center for Best Practices & Council of Chief State School Officers. (2010). *Common Core State Standards for English language arts and literacy in history/social studies, science, and technical subjects.* Authors. Accessed at https://corestandards.org/wp-content/uploads/2023/09/ELA_Standards1.pdf on March 21, 2025.

Nazari, K. B., & Ebersbach, M. (2019). Distributing mathematical practice of third and seventh graders: Applicability of the spacing effect in the classroom. *Applied Cognitive Psychology, 33*(2), 288–298. https://doi.org/10.1002/acp.3485

Nelson, T. O., & Narens, L. (1990). Metamemory: A theoretical framework and new findings. *The Psychology of Learning and Motivation, 26*, 125–173. https://doi.org/10.1016/S0079-7421(08)60053-5

Ng, Z. J., Willner, C. J., Mannweiler, M. D., Hoffmann, J. D., Bailey, C. S., & Cipriano, C. (2022). A systematic review of emotion regulation assessments in US schools: Bridging the gap between researchers and educators. *Educational Psychology Review, 34*(4), 2825–2865. https://doi.org/10.1007/s10648-022-09691-4

Nückles, M., Roelle, J., Glogger-Frey, I., Waldeyer, J., & Renkl, A. (2020). The self-regulation-view in writing-to-learn: Using journal writing to optimize cognitive load in self-regulated learning. *Educational Psychology Review, 32*(4), 1089–1126. https://doi.org/10.1007/s10648-020-09541-1

Ohtani, K., & Hisasaka, T. (2018). Beyond intelligence: A meta-analytic review of the relationship among metacognition, intelligence, and academic performance. *Metacognition and Learning, 13*(2), 179–212. https://doi.org/10.1007/s11409-018-9183-8

Omarchevska, Y., Lachner, A., Richter, J., & Scheiter, K. (2022a). Do video modeling and metacognitive prompts improve self-regulated scientific inquiry? *Educational Psychology Review, 34*(2), 1025–1061. https://doi.org/10.1007/s10648-021-09652-3

Omarchevska, Y., Lachner, A., Richter, J., & Scheiter, K. (2022b). It takes two to tango: How scientific reasoning and self-regulation processes impact argumentation quality. *Journal of the Learning Sciences, 31*(2), 237–277. https://doi.org/10.1080/10508406.2021.1966633

Onan, E., Wiradhany, W., Biwer, F., Janssen, E. M., & de Bruin, A. B. H. (2022). Growing out of the experience: How subjective experiences of effort and learning influence the use of interleaved practice. *Educational Psychology Review, 34*(4), 2451–2484. https://doi.org/10.1007/s10648-022-09692-3

Ophir, E., Nass, C., & Wagner, A. D. (2009). Cognitive control in media multitaskers. *PNAS, 106*(37), 15583–15587. https://doi.org/10.1073/pnas.0903620106

Organisation for Economic Co-operation and Development. (2023). *Education at a glance 2023: OECD indicators*. Author. Accessed at www.oecd.org/en/publications/education-at-a-glance-2023_e13bef63-en/full-report.html on April 2, 2025.

Orhan, M. A., Castellano, S., Khelladi, I., Marinelli, L., & Monge, F. (2021). Technology distraction at work. Impacts on self-regulation and work engagement. *Journal of Business Research, 126*, 341–349. https://doi.org/10.1016/j.jbusres.2020.12.048

Oudman, S., van de Pol, J., & van Gog, T. (2022). Effects of self-scoring their math problem solutions on primary school students' monitoring and regulation. *Metacognition and Learning, 17*(1), 213–239. https://doi.org/10.1007/s11409-021-09281-9

Paas, F. G. W. C., & van Merriënboer, J. J. G. (1994). Variability of worked examples and transfer of geometrical problem-solving skills: A cognitive-load approach. *Journal of Educational Psychology, 86*(1), 122–133. https://doi.org/10.1037/0022-0663.86.1.122

Pan, S. C., & Rickard, T. C. (2018). Transfer of test-enhanced learning: Meta-analytic review and synthesis. *Psychological Bulletin, 144*(7), 710–756. https://doi.org/10.1037/bul0000151

Panadero, E. (2017). A review of self-regulated learning: Six models and four directions for research. *Frontiers in Psychology, 8*, Article 422. https://doi.org/10.3389/fpsyg.2017.00422

Panadero, E., Brown, G. T. L., & Strijbos, J.-W. (2016). The future of student self-assessment: A review of known unknowns and potential directions. *Educational Psychology Review, 28*(4), 803–830. https://doi.org/10.1007/s10648-015-9350-2

Panadero, E., & Jonsson, A. (2013). The use of scoring rubrics for formative assessment purposes revisited: A review. *Educational Research Review, 9*, 129–144. http://dx.doi.org/10.1016/j.edurev.2013.01.002

Panadero, E., & Jonsson, A. (2020). A critical review of the arguments against the use of rubrics. *Educational Research Review, 30*, Article 100329. https://doi.org/10.1016/j.edurev.2020.100329

Panadero, E., Jonsson, A., & Botella, J. (2017). Effects of self-assessment on self-regulated learning and self-efficacy: Four meta-analyses. *Educational Research Review, 22*, 74–98. https://doi.org/10.1016/j.edurev.2017.08.004

Panadero, E., Jonsson, A., Pinedo, L., & Fernández-Castilla, B. (2023). Effects of rubrics on academic performance, self-regulated learning, and self-efficacy: A meta-analytic review. *Educational Psychology Review, 35*(4), Article 113. https://doi.org/10.1007/s10648-023-09823-4

Patall, E. A., Pituch, K. A., Steingut, R. R., Vasquez, A. C., Yates, N., & Kennedy, A. A. U. (2019). Agency and high school science students' motivation, engagement, and classroom support experiences. *Journal of Applied Developmental Psychology, 62*, 77–92. https://doi.org/10.1016/j.appdev.2019.01.004

Patall, E. A., Steingut, R. R., Vasquez, A. C., Trimble, S. S., Pituch, K. A., & Freeman, J. L. (2018). Daily autonomy supporting or thwarting and students' motivation and engagement in the high school science classroom. *Journal of Educational Psychology, 110*(2), 269–288. https://doi.org/10.1037/edu0000214

Pekrun, R. (2023). Jingle-jangle fallacies in motivation science: Toward a definition of core motivation. In M. Bong, J. Reeve, & S. Kim (Eds.), *Motivation science: Controversies and insights* (pp. 52–58). Oxford University Press. https://doi.org/10.1093/oso/9780197662359.003.0009

Perry, J., Lundie, D., & Golder, G. (2019). Metacognition in schools: What does the literature suggest about the effectiveness of teaching metacognition in schools? *Educational Review, 71*(4), 483–500. https://doi.org/10.1080/00131911.2018.1441127

Perry, N. E., & Rahim, A. (2011). Studying self-regulated learning in classrooms. In B. J. Zimmerman & D. H. Schunk (Eds.), *Handbook of self-regulation of learning and performance* (pp. 122–136). Routledge. https://doi.org/10.4324/9780203839010

Pintrich, P. R. (2000). The role of goal orientation in self-regulated learning. In M. Boekaerts, P. R. Pintrich, & M. Zeidner (Eds.), *Handbook of self-regulation* (pp. 451–502). Academic Press. https://doi.org/10.1016/B978-012109890-2/50043-3

Popham, W. J. (1997, October). What's wrong—and what's right—with rubrics. *Educational Leadership, 55*(2), 72–75.

Popławska, A., Szumowska, E., & Kuś, J. (2021). Why do we need media multitasking? A self-regulatory perspective. *Frontiers in Psychology, 12*, Article 624649. https://doi.org/10.3389/fpsyg.2021.624649

Potts, R., Davies, G., & Shanks, D. R. (2019). The benefit of generating errors during learning: What is the locus of the effect? *Journal of Experimental Psychology: Learning, Memory, and Cognition, 45*(6), 1023–1041. https://doi.org/10.1037/xlm0000637

Potts, R., & Shanks, D. R. (2014). The benefit of generating errors during learning. *Journal of Experimental Psychology: General, 143*(2), 644–667. https://doi.org/10.1037/a0033194

Puranik, H., Koopman, J., & Vough, H. C. (2020). Pardon the interruption: An integrative review and future research agenda for research on work interruptions. *Journal of Management, 46*(6), 806–842. https://doi.org/10.1177/0149206319887428

Puustinen, M., & Pulkkinen, L. (2001). Models of self-regulated learning: A review. *Scandinavian Journal of Educational Research, 45*(3), 269–286. https://doi.org/10.1080/00313830120074206

Raaijmakers, S. F., Baars, M., Paas, F., van Merriënboer, J., & van Gog, T. (2018). Training self-assessment and task-selection skills to foster self-regulated learning: Do trained skills transfer across domains? *Applied Cognitive Psychology, 32*(2), 270–277. https://doi.org/10.1002/acp.3392

Raaijmakers, S. F., Baars, M., Schaap, L., Paas, F., van Merriënboer, J., & van Gog, T. (2018). Training self-regulated learning skills with video modeling examples: Do task-selection skills transfer? *Instructional Science, 46*(2), 273–290. https://doi.org/10.1007/s11251-017-9434-0

Randler, C., Kranich, K., & Eisele, M. (2008). Block scheduled versus traditional biology teaching—An educational experiment using the water lily. *Instructional Science, 36*(1), 17–25.

Rapanta, C., & Iordanou, K. (2023). Argumentation and critical thinking. In R. J. Tierney, F. Rizvi, & K. Ercikan (Eds.), *International encyclopedia of education* (4th ed., pp. 575–587). Elsevier Science. https://doi.org/10.1016/B978-0-12-818630-5.14073-4

Rawson, K. A., & Dunlosky, J. (2013). Retrieval-monitoring-feedback (RMF) technique for producing efficient and durable student learning. In R. Azevedo & V. Aleven (Eds.), *International handbook of metacognition and learning technologies* (pp. 67–78). Springer.

Reddy, Y. M., & Andrade, H. (2010). A review of rubric use in higher education. *Assessment and Evaluation in Higher Education, 35*(4), 435–448. https://doi.org/10.1080/02602930902862859

Reeve, J. (2013). How students create motivationally supportive learning environments for themselves: The concept of agentic engagement. *Journal of Educational Psychology, 105*(3), 579–595. https://doi.org/10.1037/a0032690

Reeve, J., & Cheon, S. H. (2021). Autonomy-supportive teaching: Its malleability, benefits, and potential to improve educational practice. *Educational Psychologist, 56*(1), 54–77. https://doi.org/10.1080/00461520.2020.1862657

Reeve, J., Jang, H.-R., Shin, S. H., Ahn, J. S., Matos, L., & Gargurevich, R. (2022). When students show some initiative: Two experiments on the benefits of greater agentic engagement. *Learning and Instruction, 80,* Article 101564. https://doi.org/10.1016/j.learninstruc.2021.101564

Renkl, A., Stark, R., Gruber, H., & Mandl, H. (1998). Learning from worked-out examples: The effects of example variability and elicited self-explanations. *Contemporary Educational Psychology, 23*(1), 90–108. https://doi.org/10.1006/ceps.1997.0959

Rhodes, M. G. (2019). Metacognition. *Teaching of Psychology, 46*(2), 168–175. https://doi.org/10.1177/0098628319834381

Rhodes, M. G., & Tauber, S. K. (2011). The influence of delaying judgments of learning on metacognitive accuracy: A meta-analytic review. *Psychological Bulletin, 137*(1), 131–148. https://doi.org/10.1037/a0021705

Rideout, V., Peebles, A., Mann, S., & Robb, M. B. (2022). *The Common Sense census: Media use by tweens and teens, 2021* [Report]. Common Sense. Accessed at www.commonsensemedia.org/sites/default/files/research/report/8-18-census-integrated-report-final-web_0.pdf on April 2, 2025.

Rittle-Johnson, B., & Loehr, A. M. (2017). Instruction based on self-explanation. In R. E. Mayer & P. A. Alexander (Eds.), *Handbook of research on learning and instruction* (2nd ed., pp. 349–364). Routledge. https://doi.org/10.4324/9781315736419

Rivers, M. L. (2021). Metacognition about practice testing: A review of learners' beliefs, monitoring, and control of test-enhanced learning. *Educational Psychology Review, 33*(3), 823–862. https://doi.org/10.1007/s10648-020-09578-2

Roebers, C. M. (2017). Executive function and metacognition: Towards a unifying framework of cognitive self-regulation. *Developmental Review, 45,* 31–51. http://dx.doi.org/10.1016/j.dr.2017.04.001

Roebers, C. M., & Spiess, M. (2017). The development of metacognitive monitoring and control in second graders: A short-term longitudinal study. *Journal of Cognition and Development, 18*(1), 110–128. https://doi.org/10.1080/15248372.2016.1157079

Roediger, H. L., III, Agarwal, P. K., McDaniel, M. A., & McDermott, K. B. (2011). Test-enhanced learning in the classroom: Long-term improvements from quizzing. *Journal of Experimental Psychology: Applied, 17*(4), 382–395. https://doi.org/10.1037/a0026252

Roediger, H. L., III, & Karpicke, J. D. (2006a). The power of testing memory: Basic research and implications for educational practice. *Perspectives on Psychological Science, 1*(3), 181–210. https://doi.org/10.1111/j.1745-6916.2006.00012.x

Roediger, H. L., III, & Karpicke, J. D. (2006b). Test-enhanced learning: Taking memory tests improves long-term retention. *Psychological Science, 17*(3), 249–255. https://doi.org/10.1111/j.1467-9280.2006.01693.x

Rohrer, D., & Taylor, K. (2007). The shuffling of mathematics problems improves learning. *Instructional Science, 35*(6), 481–498. https://doi.org/10.1007/s11251-007-9015-8

Roscoe, R. D. (2014). Self-monitoring and knowledge-building in learning by teaching. *Instructional Science, 42*(3), 327–351. https://doi.org/10.1007/s11251-013-9283-4

Rowland, C. A. (2014). The effect of testing versus restudy on retention: A meta-analytic review of the testing effect. *Psychological Bulletin, 140*(6), 1432–1463. https://doi.org/10.1037/a0037559

Rowley, T., & McCrudden, M. T. (2020). Retrieval practice and retention of course content in a middle school science classroom. *Applied Cognitive Psychology, 34*(6), 1510–1515. https://doi.org/10.1002/acp.3710

Rutherford, T. (2017). Within and between person associations of calibration and achievement. *Contemporary Educational Psychology, 49*, 226–237. https://doi.org/10.1016/j.cedpsych.2017.03.001

Ryan, R. M., & Deci, E. L. (2000a). Intrinsic and extrinsic motivations: Classic definitions and new directions. *Contemporary Educational Psychology, 25*(1), 54–67. https://doi.org/10.1006/ceps.1999.1020

Ryan, R. M., & Deci, E. L. (2000b). Self-determination theory and the facilitation of intrinsic motivation, social development, and well-being. *American Psychologist, 55*(1), 68–78. https://doi.org/10.1037/0003-066X.55.1.68

Ryan, R. M., & Deci, E. L. (2009). Promoting self-determined school engagement: Motivation, learning, and well-being. In K. R. Wentzel & A. Wigfield (Eds.), *Handbook of motivation at school* (pp. 171–195). Routledge.

Ryan, R. M., & Deci, E. L. (2017). *Self-determination theory: Basic psychological needs in motivation, development, and wellness.* Guilford Press.

Ryan, R. M., & Deci, E. L. (2020). Intrinsic and extrinsic motivation from a self-determination theory perspective: Definitions, theory, practices, and future directions. *Contemporary Educational Psychology, 61*, Article 101860. https://doi.org/10.1016/j.cedpsych.2020.101860

Sanchez, C. E., Atkinson, K. M., Koenka, A. C., Moshontz, H., & Cooper, H. (2017). Self-grading and peer-grading for formative and summative assessments in 3rd through 12th grade classrooms: A meta-analysis. *Journal of Educational Psychology, 109*(8), 1049–1066. https://doi.org/10.1037/edu0000190

Scheiter, K., Ackerman, R., & Hoogerheide, V. (2020). Looking at mental effort appraisals through a metacognitive lens: Are they biased? *Educational Psychology Review, 32*(4), 1003–1027. https://doi.org/10.1007/s10648-020-09555-9

Schnaubert, L., Krukowski, S., & Bodemer, D. (2021). Assumptions and confidence of others: The impact of socio-cognitive information on metacognitive self-regulation. *Metacognition and Learning, 16*(3), 855–887. https://doi.org/10.1007/s11409-021-09269-5

Schneider, M., & Preckel, F. (2017). Variables associated with achievement in higher education: A systematic review of meta-analyses. *Psychological Bulletin, 143*(6), 565–600. https://doi.org/10.1037/bul0000098

Schneider, V. I., Healy, A. F., & Bourne, L. E., Jr. (1998). Contextual interference effects in foreign language vocabulary acquisition and retention. In A. F. Healy & L. E. Bourne, Jr. (Eds.), *Foreign language learning: Psycholinguistic studies on training and retention* (pp. 77–90). Erlbaum.

Schneider, V. I., Healy, A. F., & Bourne, L. E., Jr. (2002). What is learned under difficult conditions is hard to forget: Contextual interference effects in foreign vocabulary acquisition, retention, and transfer. *Journal of Memory and Language, 46*(2), 419–440. https://doi.org/10.1006/jmla.2001.2813

Schneider, V. I., Healy, A. F., Ericsson, K. A., & Bourne, L. E., Jr. (1995). The effects of contextual interference on the acquisition and retention of logical rules. In A. F. Healy & L. E. Bourne, Jr. (Eds.), *Learning and memory of knowledge and skills: Durability and specificity* (pp. 95–131). SAGE. https://doi.org/10.4135/9781483326887.n4

Schneider, W., & Löffler, E. (2016). The development of metacognitive knowledge in children and adolescents. In J. Dunlosky & S. K. Tauber (Eds.), *The Oxford handbook of metamemory* (pp. 491–518). Oxford University Press.

Schroeder, N. L., Nesbit, J. C., Anguiano, C. J., & Adesope, O. O. (2018). Studying and constructing concept maps: A meta-analysis. *Educational Psychology Review, 30*(2), 431–455. https://doi.org/10.1007/s10648-017-9403-9

Schumpe, B. M., Bélanger, J. J., Dugas, M., Erb, H.-P., & Kruglanski, A. W. (2018). Counterfinality: On the increased perceived instrumentality of means to a goal. *Frontiers in Psychology, 9*, Article 1052. https://doi.org/10.3389/fpsyg.2018.01052

Schunk, D. H., & DiBenedetto, M. K. (2016). Self-efficacy theory in education. In K. R. Wentzel & D. B. Miele (Eds.), *Handbook of motivation at school* (2nd ed., pp. 34–54). Routledge. https://doi.org/10.4324/9781315773384

Schunk, D. H., & DiBenedetto, M. K. (2020). Motivation and social cognitive theory. *Contemporary Educational Psychology, 60*, Article 101832. https://doi.org/10.1016/j.cedpsych.2019.101832

Schunk, D. H., & DiBenedetto, M. K. (2023). Learning from a social cognitive theory perspective. In R. J. Tierney, F. Rizvi, & K. Ercikan (Eds.), *International encyclopedia of education* (4th ed., pp. 22–35). Elsevier Science. https://doi.org/10.1016/B978-0-12-818630-5.14004-7

Schunk, D. H., & Usher, E. L. (2019). Social cognitive theory and motivation. In R. M. Ryan (Ed.), *The Oxford handbook of human motivation* (2nd ed., pp. 10–26). Oxford University Press. https://doi.org/10.1093/oxfordhb/9780190666453.013.2

Schuster, C., Stebner, F., Geukes, S., Jansen, M., Leutner, D., & Wirth, J. (2023). The effects of direct and indirect training in metacognitive learning strategies on near and far transfer in self-regulated learning. *Learning and Instruction, 83*, Article 101708. https://doi.org/10.1016/j.learninstruc.2022.101708

Schuster, C., Stebner, F., Leutner, D., & Wirth, J. (2020). Transfer of metacognitive skills in self-regulated learning: An experimental training study. *Metacognition and Learning, 15*(3), 455–477. https://doi.org/10.1007/s11409-020-09237-5

Schutte, G. M., Duhon, G. J., Solomon, B. G., Poncy, B. C., Moore, K., & Story, B. (2015). A comparative analysis of massed vs. distributed practice on basic math fact fluency growth rates. *Journal of School Psychology, 53*(2), 149–159. https://doi.org/10.1016/j.jsp.2014.12.003

Schwartz, J., Mochon, D., Wyper, L., Maroba, J., Patel, D., & Ariely, D. (2014). Healthier by precommitment. *Psychological Science, 25*(2), 538–546. https://doi.org/10.1177/0956797613510950

Schwieren, J., Barenberg, J., & Dutke, S. (2017). The testing effect in the psychology classroom: A meta-analytic perspective. *Psychology Learning and Teaching, 16*(2), 179–196. https://doi.org/10.1177/1475725717695149

Seabrook, R., Brown, G. D. A., & Solity, J. E. (2005). Distributed and massed practice: From laboratory to classroom. *Applied Cognitive Psychology, 19*(1), 107–122. https://doi.org/10.1002/acp.1066

Segijn, C. M., Voorveld, H. A. M., Vandeberg, L., Pennekamp, S. F., & Smit, E. G. (2017). Insight into everyday media use with multiple screens. *International Journal of Advertising, 36*(5), 779–797. https://doi.org/10.1080/02650487.2017.1348042

Shea, J. B., & Morgan, R. L. (1979). Contextual interference effects on the acquisition, retention, and transfer of a motor skill. *Journal of Experimental Psychology: Human Learning and Memory, 5*(2), 179–187. https://doi.org/10.1037/0278-7393.5.2.179

Siedlecka, M., Paulewicz, B., & Wierzchoń, M. (2016). But I was so sure! Metacognitive judgments are less accurate given prospectively than retrospectively. *Frontiers in Psychology, 7*, Article 218. https://doi.org/10.3389/fpsyg.2016.00218

Simms, J. A. (2024). *The Marzano synthesis: A collected guide to what works in K–12 education.* Marzano Resources.

Simms, J. A. (2025). *Where learning happens: Leveraging working memory & attention in the classroom.* Marzano Resources.

Simon, D. A. (2007). Contextual interference effects with two tasks. *Perceptual and Motor Skills, 105*(1), 177–183. https://doi.org/10.2466/pms.105.1.177-183

Singley, M. K., & Anderson, J. R. (1989). *The transfer of cognitive skill.* Harvard University Press.

Skinner, E. A. (2023). Four guideposts toward an integrated model of academic motivation: Motivational resilience, academic identity, complex social ecologies, and development. *Educational Psychology Review, 35*(3), Article 80. https://doi.org/10.1007/s10648-023-09790-w

Sobel, H. S., Cepeda, N. J., & Kapler, I. V. (2011). Spacing effects in real-world classroom vocabulary learning. *Applied Cognitive Psychology, 25*(5), 763–767. https://doi.org/10.1002/acp.1747

Sones, A. M., & Stroud, J. B. (1940). Review, with special reference to temporal position. *Journal of Educational Psychology, 31*(9), 665–676. https://doi.org/10.1037/h0054178

Sotola, L. K., & Crede, M. (2021). Regarding class quizzes: A meta-analytic synthesis of studies on the relationship between frequent low-stakes testing and class performance. *Educational Psychology Review, 33*(2), 407–426. https://doi.org/10.1007/s10648-020-09563-9

Spiegel, J. A., Goodrich, J. M., Morris, B. M., Osborne, C. M., & Lonigan, C. J. (2021). Relations between executive functions and academic outcomes in elementary school children: A meta-analysis. *Psychological Bulletin, 147*(4), 329–351. https://doi.org/10.1037/bul0000322

Spitzer, H. F. (1939). Studies in retention. *Journal of Educational Psychology, 30*(9), 641–656. https://doi.org/10.1037/h0063404

Stanovich, K. E. (2016). The comprehensive assessment of rational thinking. *Educational Psychologist, 51*(1), 23–34. https://doi.org/10.1080/00461520.2015.1125787

Stanovich, K. E., & West, R. F. (1997). Reasoning independently of prior belief and individual differences in actively open-minded thinking. *Journal of Educational Psychology, 89*(2), 342–357. https://doi.org/10.1037/0022-0663.89.2.342

Stebner, F., Schuster, C., Weber, X.-L., Greiff, S., Leutner, D., & Wirth, J. (2022). Transfer of metacognitive skills in self-regulated learning: Effects on strategy application and content knowledge acquisition. *Metacognition and Learning, 17*(3), 715–744. https://doi.org/10.1007/s11409-022-09322-x

Sweller, J. (2022). The role of evolutionary psychology in our understanding of human cognition: Consequences for cognitive load theory and instructional procedures. *Educational Psychology Review, 34*(4), 2229–2241. https://doi.org/10.1007/s10648-021-09647-0

Syal, S., & Nietfeld, J. L. (2022). Is situational interest a metacognitive risk? An examination of contextual factors in classroom settings. *Contemporary Educational Psychology, 71*, Article 102109. https://doi.org/10.1016/j.cedpsych.2022.102109

Szpunar, K. K., Jing, H. G., & Schacter, D. L. (2014). Overcoming overconfidence in learning from video-recorded lectures: Implications of interpolated testing for online education. *Journal of Applied Research in Memory and Cognition, 3*(3), 161–164. https://doi.org/10.1016/j.jarmac.2014.02.001

Theobald, M. (2021). Self-regulated learning training programs enhance university students' academic performance, self-regulated learning strategies, and motivation: A meta-analysis. *Contemporary Educational Psychology, 66*, Article 101976. https://doi.org/10.1016/j.cedpsych.2021.101976

Thompson, R. A. (2019). Emotion dysregulation: A theme in search of definition. *Development and Psychopathology, 31*(3), 805–815. https://doi.org/10.1017/S0954579419000282

Thorndike, E. L. (1906). *The principles of teaching: Based on psychology*. Seiler.

Thorndike, E. L. (1914). Communications and discussion. Repetition versus recall in memorizing vocabularies; The effect of continuous exercise and of rest upon difficult mental multiplication. *Journal of Educational Psychology, 5*(10), 596–599. https://doi.org/10.1037/h0072245

Thorndike, E. L. (1931). *Human learning*. Century.

Thorndike, E. L., & Woodworth, R. S. (1901). The influence of improvement in one mental function upon the efficiency of other functions. (I.). *The Psychological Review, 8*(3), 247–261.

Topping, K. J. (2024). *Improving thinking in the classroom: What works for enhancing cognition*. Routledge.

Travers, C. J., Morisano, D., & Locke, E. A. (2015). Self-reflection, growth goals, and academic outcomes: A qualitative study. *British Journal of Educational Psychology, 85*(2), 224–241. https://doi.org/10.1111/bjep.12059

Uncapher, M. R., & Wagner, A. D. (2018). Minds and brains of media multitaskers: Current findings and future directions. *PNAS, 115*(40), 9889–9896. https://doi.org/10.1073/pnas.1611612115

Urdan, T., & Kaplan, A. (2020). The origins, evolution, and future directions of achievement goal theory. *Contemporary Educational Psychology, 61*, Article 101862. https://doi.org/10.1016/j.cedpsych.2020.101862

Urhahne, D., & Wijnia, L. (2023). Theories of motivation in education: An integrative framework. *Educational Psychology Review, 35*(2), Article 45. https://doi.org/10.1007/s10648-023-09767-9

Usher, E. L. (2016). Personal capability beliefs. In L. Corno & E. M. Anderman (Eds.), *Handbook of educational psychology* (3rd ed., pp. 146–159). Routledge. https://doi.org/10.4324/9781315688244

Usher, E. L., Ford, C. J., Li, C. R., & Weidner, B. L. (2019). Sources of math and science self-efficacy in rural Appalachia: A convergent mixed methods study. *Contemporary Educational Psychology, 57*, 32–53. https://doi.org/10.1016/j.cedpsych.2018.10.003

Usher, E. L., & Schunk, D. H. (2018). Social cognitive theoretical perspective of self-regulation. In D. H. Schunk & J. A. Greene (Eds.), *Handbook of self-regulation of learning and performance* (2nd ed., pp. 19–35). Routledge. https://doi.org/10.4324/9781315697048-2

van der Graaf, J., Lim, L., Fan, Y., Kilgour, J., Moore, J., Gašević, D., et al. (2022). The dynamics between self-regulated learning and learning outcomes: An exploratory approach and implications. *Metacognition and Learning, 17*(3), 745–771. https://doi.org/10.1007/s11409-022-09308-9

van der Schuur, W. A., Baumgartner, S. E., Sumter, S. R., & Valkenburg, P. M. (2015). The consequences of media multitasking for youth: A review. *Computers in Human Behavior, 53*, 204–215. https://doi.org/10.1016/j.chb.2015.06.035

van Loon, M., de Bruin, A., Leppink, J., & Roebers, C. (2017). Why are children overconfident? Developmental differences in the implementation of accessibility cues when judging concept learning. *Journal of Experimental Child Psychology, 158*, 77–94. https://doi.org/10.1016/j.jecp.2017.01.008

Vasconcellos, D., Parker, P. D., Hilland, T., Cinelli, R., Owen, K. B., Kapsal, N., et al. (2020). Self-determination theory applied to physical education: A systematic review and meta-analysis. *Journal of Educational Psychology, 112*(7), 1444–1469. https://doi.org/10.1037/edu0000420

Veerman, M. V. M. (n.d.). *Final report TALENT EDUCATION project—Metacognition.* Talent Education. Accessed at www.talenteducation.eu/media/filer_public/9a/61/9a614052-3221-4275-9591-92b5932fe9e0/annex_ii_report_on_metacognition.pdf on April 3, 2025.

Vuorre, M., & Metcalfe, J. (2022). Measures of relative metacognitive accuracy are confounded with task performance in tasks that permit guessing. *Metacognition and Learning, 17*(2), 269–291. https://doi.org/10.1007/s11409-020-09257-1

Walton, D. (2007). *Dialog theory for critical argumentation.* Benjamins.

Wang, T., & Lajoie, S. P. (2023). How does cognitive load interact with self-regulated learning? A dynamic and integrative model. *Educational Psychology Review, 35*(3), Article 69. https://doi.org/10.1007/s10648-023-09794-6

Weinstein, C. E., Husman, J., & Dierking, D. R. (2000). Self-regulation interventions with a focus on learning strategies. In M. Boekaerts, P. R. Pintrich, & M. Zeidner (Eds.), *Handbook of self-regulation* (pp. 727–747). Academic Press. https://doi.org/10.1016/B978-012109890-2/50051-2

Weissgerber, S. C., & Rummer, R. (2023). More accurate than assumed: Learners' metacognitive beliefs about the effectiveness of retrieval practice. *Learning and Instruction, 83*, Article 101679. https://doi.org/10.1016/j.learninstruc.2022.101679

Whitebread, D., Bingham, S., Grau, V., Pino Pasternak, D., & Sangster, C. (2007). Development of metacognition and self-regulated learning in young children: Role of collaborative and peer-assisted learning. *Journal of Cognitive Education and Psychology, 6*(3), 433–455. https://doi.org/10.1891/194589507787382043

Wiley, J., & Guerrero, T. A. (2023). Fundamental processes of learning: An overview. In R. J. Tierney, F. Rizvi, & K. Ercikan (Eds.), *International encyclopedia of education* (4th ed., pp. 107–116). Elsevier Science. https://doi.org/10.1016/B978-0-12-818630-5.14014-X

Winn, A. S., DelSignore, L., Marcus, C., Chiel, L., Freiman, E., Stafford, D., et al. (2019). Applying cognitive learning strategies to enhance learning and retention in clinical teaching settings. *MedEdPORTAL, 15,* Article 10850. https://doi.org/10.15766/mep_2374-8265.10850

Winne, P. H. (2018). Cognition and metacognition within self-regulated learning. In D. H. Schunk & J. A. Greene (Eds.), *Handbook of self-regulation of learning and performance* (2nd ed., pp. 36–48). Routledge. https://doi.org/10.4324/9781315697048-3

Winne, P. H. (2022). Modeling self-regulated learning as learners doing learning science: How trace data and learning analytics help develop skills for self-regulated learning. *Metacognition and Learning, 17*(3), 773–791. https://doi.org/10.1007/s11409-022-09305-y

Wiradhany, W., & Koerts, J. (2021). Everyday functioning-related cognitive correlates of media multitasking: A mini meta-analysis. *Media Psychology, 24*(2), 276–303. https://doi.org/10.1080/15213269.2019.1685393

Wirth, J., Stebner, F., Trypke, M., Schuster, C., & Leutner, D. (2020). An interactive layers model of self-regulated learning and cognitive load. *Educational Psychology Review, 32*(4), 1127–1149. https://doi.org/10.1007/s10648-020-09568-4

Wisniewski, B., Zierer, K., & Hattie, J. (2020). The power of feedback revisited: A meta-analysis of educational feedback research. *Frontiers in Psychology, 10,* Article 3087. https://doi.org/10.3389/fpsyg.2019.03087

Wong, R. M. (2021). *Collaborative concept mapping—Meta-analysis and empirical study* [Doctoral dissertation, Washington State University]. Research Exchange. https://doi.org/10.7273/000002452

Wong, S. S. H. (2023). Deliberate erring improves far transfer of learning more than errorless elaboration and spotting and correcting others' errors. *Educational Psychology Review, 35*(1), Article 16. https://doi.org/10.1007/s10648-023-09739-z

Wong, S. S. H., & Lim, S. W. H. (2022a). Deliberate errors promote meaningful learning. *Journal of Educational Psychology, 114*(8), 1817–1831. https://doi.org/10.1037/edu0000720

Wong, S. S. H., & Lim, S. W. H. (2022b). The derring effect: Deliberate errors enhance learning. *Journal of Experimental Psychology: General, 151*(1), 25–40. https://doi.org/10.1037/xge0001072

Wylie, R., & Chi, M. T. H. (2014). The self-explanation principle in multimedia learning. In R. E. Mayer (Ed.), *The Cambridge handbook of multimedia learning* (2nd ed., pp. 413–432). Cambridge University Press. https://doi.org/10.1017/CBO9781139547369.021

Xu, Z., Zhao, Y., Liew, J., Zhou, X., & Kogut, A. (2023). Synthesizing research evidence on self-regulated learning and academic achievement in online and blended learning environments: A scoping review. *Educational Research Review, 39,* Article 100510. https://doi.org/10.1016/j.edurev.2023.100510

Yan, V. X., Bjork, E. L., & Bjork, R. A. (2016). On the difficulty of mending metacognitive illusions: A priori theories, fluency effects, and misattributions of the interleaving benefit. *Journal of Experimental Psychology: General, 145*(7), 918–933. https://doi.org/10.1037/xge0000177

Yan, Z., Wang, X., Boud, D., & Lao, H. (2023). The effect of self-assessment on academic performance and the role of explicitness: A meta-analysis. *Assessment and Evaluation in Higher Education, 48*(1), 1–15. https://doi.org/10.1080/02602938.2021.2012644

Yazdani, M. A., & Zebrowski, E., Jr. (2006). Spaced reinforcement: An effective approach to enhance the achievement in plane geometry. *Journal of Mathematical Sciences and Mathematics Education, 1*(1), 37–43.

Yeo, D. J., & Fazio, L. K. (2019). The optimal learning strategy depends on learning goals and processes: Retrieval practice versus worked examples. *Journal of Educational Psychology, 111*(1), 73–90. https://doi.org/10.1037/edu0000268

Zhang, Y., Paquette, L., Bosch, N., Ocumpaugh, J., Biswas, G., Hutt, S., et al. (2022). The evolution of metacognitive strategy use in an open-ended learning environment: Do prior domain knowledge and motivation play a role? *Contemporary Educational Psychology, 69*, Article 102064. https://doi.org/10.1016/j.cedpsych.2022.102064

Zheng, J., Lajoie, S. P., Li, S., & Wu, H. (2023). Temporal change of emotions: Identifying academic emotion trajectories and profiles in problem-solving. *Metacognition and Learning, 18*(2), 315–345. https://doi.org/10.1007/s11409-022-09330-x

Zhou, Y., & Deng, L. (2023). A systematic review of media multitasking in educational contexts: Trends, gaps, and antecedents. *Interactive Learning Environments, 31*(10), 6279–6294. https://doi.org/10.1080/10494820.2022.2032760

Zimmerman, B. J. (2013). From cognitive modeling to self-regulation: A social cognitive career path. *Educational Psychologist, 48*(3), 135–147. https://doi.org/10.1080/00461520.2013.794676

INDEX

Q

R

S

Parking Lot